McDonnell Douglas
MD-80 & MD-90

McDonnell Douglas MD-80 & MD-90

TRANS WORLD

Arthur Pearcy

MBI Publishing Company

This edition first published in 1999 by MBI Publishing Company,
729 Prospect Avenue, PO Box 1, Osceola, WI 54020-0001 USA.

Previously published by Airlife Publishing Ltd, Shrewsbury, England.

MBI Publishing Company books are also available at discounts in
bulk quantity for industrial or sales-promotional use. For details
write to Special Sales Manager at Motorbooks International Wholesalers &
Distributors, 729 Prospect Avenue, PO Box 1, Osceola, WI 54020-0001 USA.

Library of Congress Cataloging-in-Publication Data available

ISBN 0-7603-0698-2

Printed in Singapore

**Seen in picturesque European winter surroundings, MD-82 PH-MBY while under
lease to Martinair. Note the inscription on the engine nacelle reads 'DC-9 Super
80'.** *AP Photo Library*

CONTENTS

INTRODUCTION

This is the fascinating story of the latest members of the Long Beach, California family of ultra-modern airliners which today are serving airlines around the globe and will continue well into the 21st century.

Construction of the former McDonnell Douglas MD series airliners is now confirmed by new owners Boeing to continue into the year 2000, with a new model on offer to carry forward the Long Beach tradition.

$1.1trillion of world-wide investment in new airliners is projected up until the year 2015, with the world total up from 11,066 airplanes today to 23,080. From 2001 to 2005, the average investment is predicted at $50billion, and after that is expected to increase as the world airline fleet grows from 16,300 in 2005 to the 2015 total.

In the forecast world airliner fleet, products from what is now the Douglas Products Division of Boeing are included in three of the small airliners categories. The veteran DC-9-10 is listed in the 50-90 seat category, and the subjects of this book, the later MD-81/82/83/88 and the MD-90 are included in the 121-170 seat category.

The airline industry continues its recovery despite world-wide competition as new models are developed. Load factors are up and profits are on the rise. Since the jet era began, world air travel has been a growth industry. Expanding business,

BELOW: AOM's F-GGMB seen in summer 1996 livery. AOM is the major domestic carrier in Mexico, serving over 40 cities, as well as scheduled services throughout the USA and internationally across the Atlantic to Europe. The company was privatised in April 1988 after the state-owned airline, Aeronaves de Mexico, was declared bankrupt. *A P Publications*

trade, and wealth drove that trend. Looking forward two decades, the experts forecast similar air travel growth: projected traffic increase will be approximately 5.1 percent per year. More and more countries are expected to benefit from economic development and general integration into the global economy. As trade expands, businesses prosper, wealth grows, and demand for air travel increases, the future is forecast to follow much the same path as the last 20 years. World air travel will grow, faster than wealth itself.

As competition continues to intensify during the next 20 years, market forces will continue to foster change in the world's airline industry. Airlines will confront an increasingly competitive environment. Broader liberalisation of markets will continue. Long-term profitability will depend on the successful development of cost reduction strategies.

AIRLINE FLEET NEEDS CHANGE

A number of strategies, influenced by differences in traffic growth rates among major markets, will produce a marked change in the composition of the world airline fleet. With intermediate-size airplanes predicted to account for over 21 percent of the world fleet by 2015, (up from 17 percent in 1995) one can see reflected the great flexibility and increased capability offered by airline manufacturers in the form of families of intermediate-size airliners, with increasing choice between types available.

New airplane models contribute to improvements. Modern airliner families such as the Douglas/Boeing MD-80, MD-90 and MD-95 (or 717) provide design-in range capability which offers airlines operational flexibility. They offer commonality benefits which reduce crew costs. New airplanes require less

maintenance, are more reliable, and offer greatly improved fuel efficiency. Reservations can now be made on personal computer networks and savings in flight operations are also possible. Straight-line routings available from satellite-based navigation will save both time and money.

INTERMEDIATE-SIZE AIRPLANE MARKET

World market demand and airplane supply requirements appear annually in carefully researched market data documents published and circulated by most aerospace companies such as Boeing, McDonnell Douglas and Airbus Industries. The mix of new additions by 2015 will be 68 percent single-aisle, 22 percent intermediate-size and 10 percent large airplanes. The worldwide freight fleet will be 2,260 airplanes in 2015. The general indications are that the airline industry is in a state of recovery and that airline capacity is now in line with demand.

During the first half of the 1990s, the airlines were confronted by the disruptive effects of the Gulf War on economic growth and air travel. At the same time, they were introducing large amounts of new capacity. The combination of slow growth and this increase in capacity led to significant industry operating losses. However, by 1993 the airlines began recording operating profits, and by 1995 they had increased year-over-year orders for new airplanes for the first time in the decade.

The early 1990s can best be characterised by the imbalance between capacity and demand. The slowdown in the world economic growth coincided with the delivery of a record number of airliners. Airlines had ordered these planes during the boom years of the late 1980s, but by 1990 excess capacity existed within the industry. The number of parked airplanes in desert outposts located at Mojave, California and Kingman, Arizona, reflects the magnitude of this excess, doubling from 500 in 1990 to 1,000 (or even more) in 1991. This parked fleet grew to 1,110 over the next two years.

However, by 1995 this same parked fleet had decreased by more than 370 airplanes, leaving approximately 730 in the desert park by the end of the year. Based on historic levels in relation to the total world fleet, at least 275 are needed to support the used airplane market. These are 26 or even more years old, and are expected to return to active airline service as an alternative to new factory airplanes.

NOISE

Noise deadlines are having a severe effect on the airliner order outlook. Legislative requirements to retire or make quiet is known as Stage 2 airplanes, this introduces uncertainty into the near-term outlook for airplane orders, primarily from Europe and the USA. These requirements encompass a large number of airplanes — 3,600 worldwide in 1995. Airlines face three choices: they can replace with new airplanes; they can hushkit or re-engine old airplanes; or they can remove the offending airplanes from the fleet and not replace them. Which choices are made by the different airline companies will affect airline capacity and orders over the next five years.

Indications are that European airlines will not hushkit airplanes as extensively as US operators. Individual airports in

Europe have more influence in determining noise and emission requirements. To complicate matters, some selected airports specifically exclude hushkitted airplanes, making fleet planning more difficult.

Half of the US Stage 2 airplanes will be hushkitted making the USA the primary potential market. At the end of 1995 there were 2,090 airplanes in the US Stage 2 fleet. Already 13 percent are hushkitted to meet Stage 3 requirements. The current projection — based on the announced intention of the airlines — is that another 35 percent will be hushkitted. However the balance of the fleet is forecast to be replaced primarily because of age. The MD series airliners are well placed to take advantage of this situation.

AIR TRAVEL

World air travel is forecast to grow by 70 percent in 10 years. By 2005, airlines will need to carry 2,700 billion revenue passenger miles per year, and — though recent economic problems may change the outlook — economic and travel growth from the Asia-Pacific region has been forecast to dominate. The world commercial jet fleet capacity should reach 3,600 billion available seat miles by 2005. This air travel growth drives the demand for more capacity and additional airplanes.

The world airline fleet mix continues to change, while airlines select the airplane size and range combination that suits their strategies and minimises financial risk. To prosper in a very competitive marketplace, airlines will increasingly select fleets which give them the flexibility they need to serve their markets — which is why two thirds of the airplanes expected to be required over the next 20 years will be single-aisle types.

The very detailed monthly *Douglas Aircraft Inventory Status* for June 1996 lists 875 DC-9s in service with 71 operators, 1,138 MD-80s with 55 operators and 17 MD-90s with four operators. By March 1997 there were still 869 DC-9s operated by those 71 operators, while 1,135 MD-80s were being flown by 56 operators and the MD-90 had increased to 46 with 10 airlines. It is historically interesting to recall that a total of 976 airliners in the DC-9 series were built, the last one, a DC-9-32 for the US Navy being delivered on 28 October 1982.

Today, single-aisle airlines dominate short flights. The current world fleet of 8,200 single-aisle airplanes is expected to increase to 11,700 by the year 2005. The utilisation of single-aisle airliners will possibly decline from today's share of 74 percent to 72 percent, or even lower, of the world fleet. Despite the need for large numbers of single-aisle airplanes, their share of the world fleet declines. Markets served by these airliners are possibly not growing as rapidly as markets where larger airplanes predominate.

RIGHT: One of American Airline's fleet of MD-80 series airliners departing into a storm-ridden sky. Today AA operates the largest airline fleet of any single type in the world outside the CIS. By July 1997 American operated 234 MD-82s and 26 MD-83s on its extensive route system across the USA. There was a time when, if all its commitments to the MD-80 series had been exercised, the fleet could have reached a staggering 350 twin-jet airliners. *AF Photo Library*

ASIA-PACIFIC

Single-aisle airliners in the Asia-Pacific area are concentrated on domestic routes. Because of the area's geography they make up a small share of the regional fleets. In the same areas, regional flows are longer haul, and airport capacity is constrained. As a result of this, though the region accounts for 14 percent of world revenue passenger miles, it accounts for only 9 percent of the world's single-aisle fleet. Subsequently these airplanes will continue to provide a smaller share of capacity in the Asia-Pacific area than those in Europe and North America, being used for shorter regional markets and for domestic flights.

The exception will be China, where it is forecast that rapid traffic growth and system expansion will drive the requirements. There air travel is expected to increase at nearly twice the Asia-Pacific average and, consequently, China's domestic market will be among the world's largest markets for single-aisle airliners over the next two decades.

There is no doubt that the domestic United States is the world's largest market for both air travel and single-aisle airliners. Deregulation some 17 years ago dramatically changed airplane requirements. Linear route structures changed to efficient hub-and-spoke networks, (although not all US airlines have developed hub-and-spoke systems) with hub carriers offering the frequencies needed to dominate spoke cities. As hubs are expanded, smaller cities can be added, increasing regional dominance. These frequency-orientated strategies shifted airplane requirements from larger, low seat-mile cost airliners to smaller types with low trip costs. Ageing wide-body airplanes have been perceived as financially risky, thus most of the remaining wide-body fleet has been transferred to international services, sold, or parked in desert storage.

EUROPE

Travel within Europe is the second largest market for single-aisle airliners. Historically routes between most European cities were flown cooperatively by the two national flag airlines and domestic markets were often monopolies for the national airline. European airlines generally met their need for increased capacity with larger airplanes, similar to the USA before deregulation. Recently, liberalisation has opened up the European market by limited market sharing agreements. The airlines are revising their strategies; major airlines are adding new routes from their primary hubs and adding frequencies on established routes. Competitive pressures comparable to those the US airlines experienced are being felt in Europe. Many are reducing the number of twin-aisle airplanes in their short-haul fleets and adding single-aisle airliners. Continued liberalisation in Eastern Europe will surely lead to more competitors in many markets.

The introduction of high-speed rail services is likely to cause a decline in air travel to some capitals in Europe. This will lessen the requirement for twin-aisle airliners. Charter airlines carry approximately half of intra-European traffic and account for about a third of the airplanes. These airlines require airplanes that combine low seat-mile costs, low trip costs, and good field performance and range capability. It is forecast their needs will continue to be best met with the slightly larger single-aisle models.

Intermediate-size airplanes should be the fastest growing segment of the market for commercial airplanes. There are two reasons for this. First, these airplanes are gaining in range capacity. This allows them to serve more inter-continental markets. Second, regional traffic growth will drive markets served with larger single-aisle airplanes up to intermediate-size. Over the next decade, the share of intermediate-size airplanes is projected to increase from 17 to 19 percent. A total of 1,460 deliveries are projected over this 10 year period.

Arthur Pearcy

1 EVOLUTION

THE DC PEDIGREE

During the annual Douglas Aircraft Company stockholders' meeting held during April 1966, just days before Boeing announced the first order for its 747, an official of the California-based company confidently stated that it was in 'one of the most satisfactory phases of its 47 years' history.' He was, in fact, entirely mistaken.

Faced with rising costs, labour shortages, delays in delivery by key suppliers and the urgent need to expand its production facilities, the Douglas company lost control of its costs. Earnings which had been expected to reach about $20million during the fiscal year 1966, gave place to a deficit, after tax credits of $27,330,067. With a substantial backlog of orders, the company had hoped to obtain sufficient additional working capital and, while attempts were made to raise $50m of equity capital,

Douglas negotiated with its bankers for an increase in its credit. Following the bankers' advice, Douglas then approached the Wall Street firm of Lazard Fréres to obtain assistance in finding a solution to the problem.

Lazard Fréres moved into Douglas's Santa Monica plant, and used it as a headquarters in order to assist in sorting out various offers of financial assistance and direct merger. On 9 December 1966 Lazard Fréres made it clear that, in their professional opinion, a company merger was necessary and that what Douglas needed was not only capital but also a new management. Merger offers were received during the next few weeks from Fairchild, General Dynamics, Martin Marietta, McDonnell, North American Aviation and Signal Oil & Gas.

From these offers, that made by McDonnell of St. Louis, Missouri, was unanimously recommended on 13 January 1967,

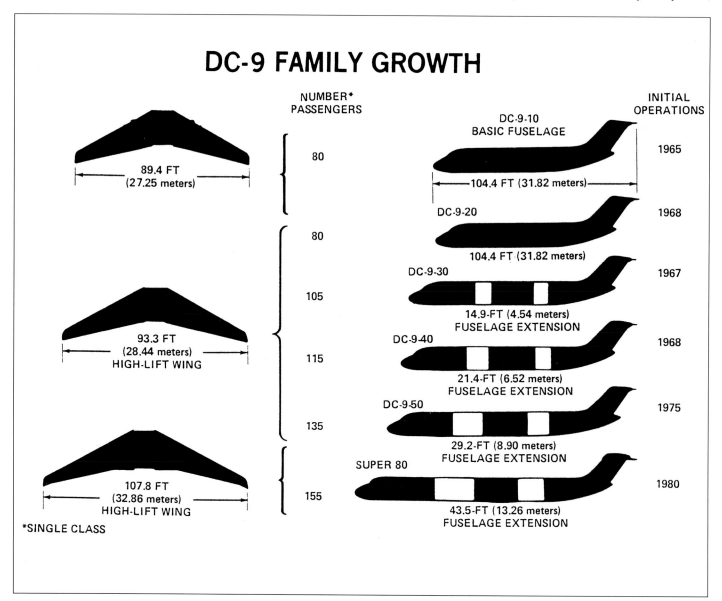

*SINGLE CLASS

by the joint negotiating committee Douglas had set up along with Lazard Fréres to advise the Board of Directors of the ailing company. The offer made by the McDonnell Company consisted of the immediate purchase of $68,700,000 of 1.5 million new Douglas common shares and then, should the proposed merger be approved by the US Justice Department, all shares of Douglas stock would be exchanged for one and three-quarter shares of McDonnell common stock.

Its is interesting to reflect that four years earlier, James S. McDonnell, Chairman of the McDonnell company, had acquired 300,000 shares of Douglas common stock. He approached both Donald W. Douglas Snr and Donald Douglas Jnr with a merger proposal, offering one share of McDonnell stock for two shares of Douglas common stock, but the plan was soundly rejected.

But in 1967, US government approval followed swiftly, as continuation of operations by the Douglas Company was important to sustain the war effort in Vietnam and, on 28 April, the Douglas Aircraft Company Inc. gave its name to the McDonnell Douglas Corporation — MDC.

LONG BEACH

The new MDC management brought a backlog of DC-9 deliveries back on schedule, and the airliner kept its hard-won status as the world's best-selling twin-jet airliner through the early 1970s.

The DC-9's history was tied up with that of the famous Douglas plant at Long Beach. Taking advantage of a huge World War 2 aircraft building programme launched by the US government, Douglas had organised a wholly-owned subsidiary, Western Land Improvement Co. which undertook the construction of a new plant adjacent to the Long Beach Municipal Airport. During November 1941 the new Long Beach plant was

ready to begin operation and the first aircraft constructed there was a Douglas C-47-DL Skytrain, delivered on 23 December, 1941, just 16 days after the United States entered the war.

In June 1955, Douglas had announced itself ready to enter the jet transport world, and was rewarded on 25 October when Pan American World Airways announced an initial order for 25 DC-8 airliners. For the first 11 months after that historic order, the Douglas DC-8 order book was ahead of that for the Boeing 707.

However, the facilities at Douglas's Santa Monica plant were inadequate for the company expansion that was required. The runway was far too short and it was surrounded by a residential area that opposed major noise disturbance. Capitalising on its existing facilities at Long Beach, and on the willingness of the municipality to enlarge, the Douglas company announced in April 1956 the construction of new facilities on a 55-acre site adjacent to the existing plant on the other side of Lakewood Boulevard. It was initially intended only to house the new DC-8 production line, and was anticipated to cost $19million complete with all the fittings and machinery. The actual cost proved much higher — in 1957 alone the company spent some $30,800,000 for property, equipment etc. This amount just exceeded the net income of $30,665,252 realised during that year.

The new building consisted of two large production halls, linked by a central core of offices and covering a grand total of 1.14m sq ft, over 26-acres. The west hall — 1,144ft long, 480ft wide and 57ft high — was for major sub-assembly, fabrication of wings, fuselage barrels, cockpits etc. It contained three bays spanning 160ft each. The east hall was the same length but the height was 67ft with two bays 160ft and 200ft wide respectively accommodating a 12-position assembly line for the DC-8. After the aircraft passed the sixth position it was transported outdoors, where the fuselage was pressure-tested to 12.33psi (lb per sq in) then returned to the assembly line. May 1957 was the target date for building completion and a further addition was a separate facility erected nearby for painting the airliners' exterior.

While both Douglas and Boeing were developing their respective commercial jets, the world's airlines had been experiencing a period of rapid growth. There were increases in passenger-miles of 17.3 percent in 1955, 16.4 percent in 1956 and 14.7 percent in 1957, while the economy of the nations in the western hemisphere was progressing rapidly. However, when the Boeing 707-120 and the Douglas DC-8-10 entered service in October 1958 and September 1959, respectively, airline traffic had slumped with the passenger miles growth rate being only 4.9 percent. This resulted in follow-on orders for both the Boeing 707 and Douglas DC-8 not reaching their anticipated rate.

Both airliners initially failed to achieve their guaranteed range, resulting in further funds being spent to correct the deficiency. The problems resulted in a sharp reduction in DC-8 sales from 73 in 1955, to 40 in 1956, 10 in 1957, 11 in 1958, 18 in 1959 and only three in 1960. Net income of the company unfortunately kept dropping, from the second highest profit figure of $33,202,304 achieved in 1956, to $16,847,028 in 1958. This was the year during which the company recorded its all time net sales record of $1,209,920,338. In 1959 it recorded its second net loss of $33,822,229. Douglas again recorded a net loss in 1960, of $19,429,437, but profitability returned in 1961 when a net income of $5,956,909 was achieved.

TWIN-JET STUDY

The market data research division of Douglas was busy reviewing a potential market for a short-range jet airliner, and had in fact commenced a series of design studies of the type. It was February 1963, after a net profit of $10,205,248 had been achieved in 1962, that the Douglas management authorised detailed engineering work on the design of a twin-jet airliner, and in May 1963 the sale of 15 new airliners known as the DC-9 was announced to Delta Air Lines.

Production of the DC-9 was conceived as an original risk-sharing programme involving other manufacturers in an intricate network of plants. The nose of the airliner was built at Santa Monica, the wing and tail assemblies by de Havilland of Canada, fuselage panels by Aerfer in Italy, whilst various other

RIGHT: The parallel final assembly lines at Long Beach plant during 1986 when the DC-8 and DC-9 were in production. Today the same huge building is occupied with the final assembly of both the MD-80 and MD-90 Series of twin-jet airliners. Swissair is one of the companies oldest customers dating back to the 1930s when it purchased Douglas DC-2s which were sub-assembled by Fokker. *MDC*

components were manufactured in the USA. The Long Beach plant was responsible for the production of the fuselage and final assembly. Initially this operation took place on a single assembly line producing jointly the DC-8 and the DC-9. The DC-9 achieved great success and in 1965 alone 170 of the twin-jet airliners were sold and by the end of 1966 total sales reached 424 aircraft.

What was initially a joint DC-8, DC-9 production line at Long Beach was replaced by a single DC-8 production line and two parallel DC-9 lines. A new subsidiary, Douglas Aircraft Company of Canada assumed responsibility for the production of both wing and tail assemblies for the DC-9. Douglas leased and operated portions of the de Havilland (Canada) plant located at Malton, Ontario with effect from 1 December 1965.

By the spring of 1978, sales of the Douglas DC-9 series airliner had reached 976, with the last a military Series 32-C9 BuNo 161530 completed on 26 August 1982, f/n 1084 s/n 48166, being delivered to the US Navy on 28 October.

Any further orders came under the new nomenclature DC-9 Super 80, or DC-9-80 — later this airliner was called MD-80, and so a new airliner family (or at least a new generation) began.

TOP: The competition — the Boeing 737, the most successful jet of all time. This is a Boeing 737-300, a series that went into production in March 1981. A re-engined 737-200, it had structural and aerodynamic improvements adapted from the Boeing 757 and 767. The JT8D-engines were replaced by larger CFM-56 engines using a redesigned nacelle. Here at San Francisco on 26 July 1995 is Western Pacific 737-301 N303AU which first flew on 15 May 1985. The paint scheme features the popular cartoon *The Simpsons*. *Ed Davies*

ABOVE: An historic photograph taken on 30 July 1988 at Long Beach showing TWA MD-83 N9304C, s/n 49530 f/n 1397, with vintage DC-2 NC13940 also in TWA livery from the Douglas Historical Foundation. The airline, then Trans Continental & Western Air, received its first DC-2 on 14 May 1934. By March 1997 TWA was operating a total of 30 MD-82 and 24 MD-83 airliners plus no less than 58 of the earlier DC-9 series. *Douglas*

ABOVE RIGHT: Stablemate of the MD-80 and MD-90 was the stretched DC-10 — the MD-11. Its launch had been frustrated by a sharp fall in airline traffic and internal problems at Long Beach. It was 17 months before sufficient orders were obtained from a dozen airlines to enable the MD-11 programme to be launched on 30 December 1986. Depicted is the 47th MD-11, N311MD, which first flew on 26 April 1990. An MDC release dated August 1997 claimed 32 customers in 24 countries with 372 commitments. However, by December 1997 the MD-11 was only serving 21 customers, operating a total of 171 aircraft. *Douglas*

RIGHT: Between 1965 and 1982 a total of 976 DC-9s was built at the Long Beach plant, the last being delivered on 28 October 1982. Depicted is the fourth DC-9, N3303L, completed for Delta Air Lines on 24 May 1965. *Douglas*

2 DESIGN

DESIGNING THE 'SUPER 80'

Each succeeding airliner design has to fly more safely and more efficiently that its predecessors. Each innovation that introduces better performance to aircraft normally results in more work and more complex systems for engineers to design. Today they are helped by computers, which permit rapid and accurate analyses of proposed aircraft changes and improvements. New tools enable designers to check more aspects of each design than was possible before, but the engineers' workload remains about the same.

However, the combined and concerted effort of a large team of design specialists was required to produce a major new derivative such as the DC-9 Super 80 airliner. With the first prototype scheduled for flight testing in mid-1979, approximately 500 engineers were employed in designing the many new systems and components which distinguished the Super 80 from its predecessors.

At MDC the team were involved in determining what elements the customers desire in an aircraft, before assessing the feasibility of producing the new design. Market data research was heavily involved in forecasting the world needs over the next few decades as regards airline growth and demand. The team also had to decide what to change and what to retain in the new design.

With 976 DC-9s already delivered by 1982, the company planners had plenty of ideas supported by the reliability of the basic DC-9 design before they commenced the task of designing the Super 80. In reviewing feedback from the many airliners and operators, apparently several themes were continually repeated. The need for a more economical, more fuel-efficient and much quieter airliner in the DC-9 category that could carry more passengers was most often expressed. Determining that one could be built with the required range and economies was the task of MDC Advanced Engineering.

ADVANCED DESIGN

Over several months a relatively small team of advanced engineers studied the many potential configurations. After looking at a number of possible fuselage enlargements, the engineers concluded that a 14.3ft (4.36m) 'stretch' over the DC-9 series 50 was optimum for increasing passenger and cargo capacity and lowering direct operating costs.

They determined that if the new, quieter, Pratt & Whitney JT8D-209 engine would be ready in time it would meet both noise and performance guarantees. Higher take-off gross weight was a requirement to give the Super 80 the desired range with its increased payload.

The designers also knew that a wing change would be necessary in the new airliner. A particularly significant and deep study involved the potential benefit of using a super-critical wing on an improved DC-9. Because the Super 80 was not a long-range aircraft, the study team concluded that the super-critical wing was not cost-effective, so its benefits did not justify inclusion in the new Super 80 design. Instead they determined that adding to the wing root and wing tip as well as improving the simple and efficient DC-9 high-lift system, would provide at reasonable cost, the increased fuel capacity, and range they were seeking.

A wing root enlargement was designed to increase the Super 80's wing area and fuel capacity. A 2ft wing tip extension was added to increase the wing aspect ratio of the DC-9 to aid performance. Larger trailing-edge flaps were designed for lower stall speeds, plus an immediate extension position for the leading edge slats for low drag on take-off and for better climb out characteristics at the Super 80's higher gross weight. The improved high-lift system, the wing area and the more powerful new engine were planned to enhance the performance of the new Super 80. Combined with the larger fan of the 'dash 209' engine which would reduce noise as well as aid performance, these features alone would dramatically reduce the noise impact on hostile areas in the vicinity of airports.

The DC-9 Super 80 was forecast to be the quietest commercial jet-liner when it went into service during 1980. Once the advanced designer had achieved a basic Super 80 configuration and performance profile, a huge marketing effort was launched worldwide to assess the chance for success. Results showed high interest in the Super 80 with an excellent market potential. On this basis and with sufficient initial orders in hand, the MDC management announced the start of the Super 80 programme in October 1977. Even before then, company engineers were planning for an orderly transition from Advanced to Design Engineering.

DETAILED DESIGN

Detailed designs based on concepts developed by advanced designers had to be prepared. Super 80 Chief Design Engineer Mike O'Connor coordinated the work required of engineering specialists in structure, aerodynamics, avionics, environmental

ABOVE RIGHT: The MD-80 flight test crew go on board N980DC for its first flight on 18 October 1979. The 909th twin-jet airliner off the Long Beach assembly line, it flew from Long Beach to Yuma, Arizona, where MDC had its flight test facilities. Flight trials proceeded smoothly until 17 December when the airliner ran into problems during a departure stall manoeuvre. MDC

RIGHT: With the prototype MD-80 in the background, the flight test crew are seen posing prior to first flight. Chief Engineering Pilot H. H. 'Knick' Knickerbocker, in the centre, was involved with the new airliner programme from its inception. Virginia 'Ginny' A. Clare was the 'Super 80' flight test engineer and John Lane the project pilot. MDC

systems, power plant, mechanical, human factors, materials and process, interiors and structures analysis, who were working with advanced design engines so that they would be ready to assume responsibility once the Super 80 programme was launched.

It was up to these specialists to turn the preliminary design theories into 'nuts and bolts' engineering drawings. More than 3,000 such drawings were required for the Super 80. Translating something from an idea to a drawing is not easy. Sometimes the cycle has to be repeated several times before the design is finalised. Once released, each drawing must then be reviewed by tooling, planning and manufacturing specialists who decided what tools must be made to produce the new part and how the new part or system is to be integrated into the manufacturing process.

Design feasibility is reviewed at a variety of points:

1. By the check group at the drawing stage.
2. In the construction of system mock-ups for complex new areas.
3. By the computer-aided design techniques.
4. By planning and tooling people who catch fit or 'go-together' problems.

Once parts are built they are subject to many tests, which sometimes result in redesign.

Finally, in the prototype Super 80 flight tests, other engineering improvements were suggested. Four key men in advanced design of the new airliner were RT Cathers, Principal Configuration Engineer; AJ Testa, Senior Configuration Engineer; HC Funk, DC-9 Project Engineer; and CJ Shepard, Project Configuration Engineer.

Thousands of working hours by hundreds of MDC engineers were required to produce the Super 80. Add to that the thousands of hours involved in simulation and the testing required for new designs. Senior engineers with hundreds of man-years of experience supervised the new design, many of whom had been heavily involved with the successful design of the DC-9 since its inception. This engineering innovation and diligence plus the input from millions of hours of DC-9 operation were combined to ensure that the Super 80 would maintain the enviable passenger appeal, profit potential and reliability of the DC-9 family.

ABOVE LEFT: Wind tunnel tests on a 9% scale model of the MD-87 twin-jet airliner undergoing low-speed testing in the United Technologies Research Center wind tunnel at Longueuil, Quebec, Canada. Standard on the MD-87 was the 10in (25.4cm) extension to the vertical stabiliser to retain the excellent handling characteristics of the MD-80 series. Also shown is the redesigned extended tail cone standard on all MD-80s as from 1986. It reduces drag and saves fuel. *MDC*

CENTRE LEFT: The MD-80 has a longer fuselage and greater wingspan than previous DC-9 series, carrying up to 172 passengers. The aircraft is registered N980DC. *MDC*

LEFT: The DC-9 'Super 80' seen on one of its test flights. When it entered airline service in October 1980 it became the quietest jet airliner in the skies. Its operating costs and fuel consumption per passenger continue to be the lowest of any aircraft in its class. *MDC*

MODELS

A low-speed wind-tunnel model underwent a series of tests for the Super 80 in the 12ft wind-tunnel at the National Aeronautics and Space Administration's (NASA) Ames Research Center located south of San Francisco, to determine how well the new airliner would meet its design objectives. Data collected from Ames and other wind-tunnel tests certainly paid off with improvements and modifications to produce more capacity, lower noise levels, good economics and reduced fuel consumption.

A wind-tunnel model can cost upwards from several hundred thousand dollars, and is built to determine how the real airliner will function in take-off, landing and cruise configurations. High-speed models are made almost entirely of metal with sensors to determine cruise performance. Low-speed models have movable surfaces such as flaps and ailerons to simulate take-offs, landings and other flight phases. Testing at low speeds is also conducted with flutter models; these are built of balsa wood and fibreglass over aluminium spars. Weight distribution in the models simulates conditions anticipated in the real aircraft.

During testing, the flutter models are exposed to a constant airflow, but are jolted or excited to test the damping characteristics of the design. Wind-tunnel models range from relatively simple preliminary models for use early in the programme, to highly sophisticated models which obtain and confirm final design details. Experience has shown that a high degree of correlation exists between wind tunnel tests and flight tests in full-scale aircraft. In all more than 1,500 hours of Super 80 testing were completed. A similar programme was coordinated for the later MD-90 and MD-95, all derivatives of the successful Super 80, known today as the MD-80.

HISTORY OF STRETCH

With the exception of the enigmatic DC-5, the trend with each and every model of Douglas Commercial transports was to be larger than its predecessor. This long lasting tradition of stretching the fuselages of its airliners' goes back to 1934 when the original 12-seat Douglas DC-1 (Douglas Commercial) was stretched into the 14-seat DC-2. This was followed by that of the DC-4 into the DC-6 during 1946, the DC-6A in 1949, DC-7 in 1953 and DC-7C in 1955 at the end of the propliner era. One must not forget the ubiquitous DC-3 which was re-built as a Super DC-3, with stretch, in 1948.

By the mid-1970s the MDC subsidiary in Long Beach, (still known and respected as the Douglas Aircraft Company) had become the almost undisputed champion of capacity increase through fuselage lengthening. The company was keen to retain its privileged role as the world's leading supplier of commercial transport aircraft and a challenge from Seattle with the Boeing 367-80 prototype jet transport could not be ignored. On 30 May 1958, the first Douglas DC-8 flew. Eight years later, in 1966, came the stretched DC-8 with the long Series 60.

By this time the first Douglas DC-9, a Series 10, had flown on 25 February 1965. This family of successful twin-jet airliners immediately became the subject of stretching by the company. The Series 10 which was 104ft 5in (31.82m) long was stretched to 119ft 5in (36.39m) to become the Series 30 in 1966. It was further stretched to 125ft 7in (38.27m) to become the Series 40 in 1967, and then stretched to 133ft 7in (40.71m) to become the Series 50 in 1974. Overall length and maximum certificated seating capacity had been increased 26.4 percent and 54.4 percent over corresponding figures for the initial DC-9-10.

The DC-9-50 was already representing a far greater stretch than had previously been achieved with other airliners, but the Long Beach design team knew that the successful DC-9 could be stretched even further to achieve still better seat mile costs. However, at this time an increasing concern over all forms of air pollution was activating most regulatory agencies in the United States to plan stricter regulations on noise and air pollution in general. The MDC design engineers also knew that another stretch of the DC-9 fuselage would either entail a significant reduction in range, or require quieter and cleaner engines. Fortunately for the future of the DC-9, and as it later

turned out, for the future of the Long Beach production line of airliners, timely development by Pratt & Whitney of refanned versions of their successful JT8D turbofan series opened up a complete new line of development.

FLIGHT TESTING

When the prototype MD-80 first flew on 18 October 1979, it had a unique flight test engineering crew on board. Chief Engineering Pilot H. H. 'Knick' Knickerbocker was pilot-in-command. He had been involved with the MD-80, or DC-9 Super 80, programme since its inception. He joined Long Beach in October 1953 later becoming Project Engineering Test Pilot for the DC-9 Series 50 and supervised all flight operation activities relating to engineering flight test for both commercial and military programmes.

John P. Laine was the DC-9 Super 80 (MD-80) Project Pilot. He joined the company in May 1966, completing the DC-9 ground school, flight and instructor pilots course earning an

Airline Transport Pilot's certificate with a rating on the DC-9. As an engineering test pilot he flew the DC-9-50 flyover noise project, DC-9 NASA Refan programme, DC-9-50 certification programme, and DC-9 runway development programme.

Flight Test Engineer for the MD-80 was Virginia 'Ginny' A. Clare, who joined Long Beach in January 1969 as aerospace engineer on the DC-10 programme. In June 1979 she was assigned flight engineer to the prototype MD-80, after being promoted in May 1978 to the position of flight test engineer with flying status.

The engineering flight test trio, along with many others were involved with the new airliner from the day the decision was made at Long Beach to produce the MD-80 on 20 October 1977. It was then known as the DC-9 Super 80. Production began in 1978 with the machining of the first wing spar, and assembly of the initial nose section was underway by November 1978. The maiden flight on 18 October 1979 lasted 2hr 50mins. The flight test programme that followed leading to certification involved some 1,085 hours of flying time. The new airliner was certificated by the FAA on 25 August 1980 with first delivery to an airline taking place on 12 September 1980 and the new MD-80 entered commercial service on 5 October 1980.

The first flight of the MD-90 took place on 22 February 1993 with N901DC f/n 2018 s/n 53367, the flight crew being Chief Test Pilot William Jones, Test Pilot G R 'Bear' Smith, and Flight Test Engineer Barry McCarthy. Other Long Beach based flight test teams included John I Miller and Douglas Moss, both engineering test pilots who have been involved in several first flights of MDC aircraft. Tom Melody is another engineering test pilot involved in MD-87 and MD-88 certification programmes. Fred Schreiner, Jack Boman and John Groves, have all logged many flight test hours including production and test flight engineering programmes.

BELOW: The DC-9 'Super 80' lifts off the runway at Long Beach on its maiden flight on 18 October 1979. Later designated MD-80, it was heralded as the first of the new technology jet airliners. *MDC*

3 PRODUCTION

As has already been discussed, when McDonnell and Douglas merged, it was decided that the facilities at Douglas's Santa Monica plant were inadequate for the company expansion that was required. The runway was far too short and it was surrounded by a residential area that opposed major noise disturbance. Capitalising on its existing facilities at Long Beach, and on the willingness of the municipality to enlarge, the Douglas company announced in April 1956 the construction of new facilities on a 55-acre site adjacent to the existing plant on the other side of Lakewood Boulevard.

The new building consisted of two large production halls, linked by a central core of offices and covering a grand total of 1.14m sq ft, over 26-acres. The west hall — 1,144ft long, 480ft wide and 57ft high — was for major sub-assembly, fabrication of wings, fuselage barrels, cockpits etc. It contained three bays spanning 160ft each. The east hall was the same length but the height was 67ft with two bays 160ft and 200ft wide respectively accommodating a 12-position assembly line for the DC-8. This is where the MD-80 and MD-90 are put together, although, as is usual these days, the components come from far and wide.

MDC CHINA PROGRAMME

An historic aviation co-production agreement was signed in April 1985 linking McDonnell Douglas Corporation and the General Administration of Civil Aviation of China (CAAC) in an interesting series of activities.

RIGHT: Photo taken in Building 13, the original assembly hall for both the DC-9 and the MD-80 series. Prior to 1994 the fuselage was built panel-by-panel; the MD-80 panels being manufactured by Alenia of Italy before shipping to the USA for assembly at Long Beach. In 1994 the method of construction changed to the 'barrel' method and now the panels are assembled into circular sections at the MDC Salt Lake City, Utah, facility and shipped to Long Beach for mating in the huge Building 80. *MDC*

BELOW RIGHT: Being prepared for delivery to airlines around the globe, factory new MD-80 twin-jets and MD-11 trijet aircraft are seen parked on the flight ramp at Long Beach during April 1990. The first three are MD-88s in Delta livery, whilst two more await their paint to be applied. Each new airliner is test flown as required by both MDC and airline pilots before being accepted for delivery. *MDC*

BELOW: Graphic of MD-80 series component manufacturers. *MDC*

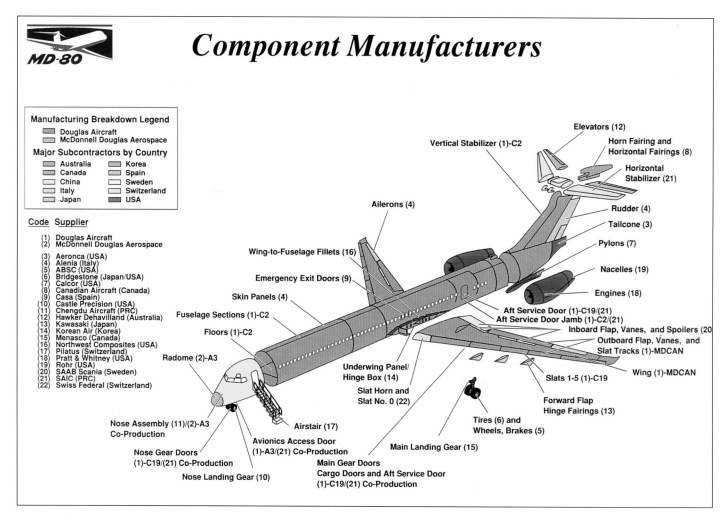

Component Manufacturers

MD-80

Manufacturing Breakdown Legend
- Douglas Aircraft
- McDonnell Douglas Aerospace

Major Subcontractors by Country
- Australia
- Canada
- China
- Italy
- Japan
- Korea
- Spain
- Sweden
- Switzerland
- USA

Code Supplier
(1) Douglas Aircraft
(2) McDonnell Douglas Aerospace
(3) Aeronca (USA)
(4) Alenia (Italy)
(5) ABSC (USA)
(6) Bridgestone (Japan/USA)
(7) Calcor (USA)
(8) Canadian Aircraft (Canada)
(9) Casa (Spain)
(10) Castle Precision (USA)
(11) Chengdu Aircraft (PRC)
(12) Hawker Dehavilland (Australia)
(13) Kawasaki (Japan)
(14) Korean Air (Korea)
(15) Menasco (Canada)
(16) Northwest Composites (USA)
(17) Pilatus (Switzerland)
(18) Pratt & Whitney (USA)
(19) Rohr (USA)
(20) SAAB Scania (Sweden)
(21) SAIC (PRC)
(22) Swiss Federal (Switzerland)

Elevators (12)
Horn Fairing and Horizontal Fairings (8)
Horizontal Stabilizer (21)
Vertical Stabilizer (1)-C2
Rudder (4)
Tailcone (3)
Ailerons (4)
Pylons (7)
Wing-to-Fuselage Fillets (16)
Nacelles (19)
Emergency Exit Doors (9)
Engines (18)
Skin Panels (4)
Aft Service Door (1)-C19/(21)
Aft Service Door Jamb (1)-C2/(21)
Fuselage Sections (1)-C2
Inboard Flap, Vanes, and Spoilers (20)
Floors (1)-C2
Outboard Flap, Vanes, and Slat Tracks (1)-MDCAN
Radome (2)-A3
Slats 1-5 (1)-C19
Wing (1)-MDCAN
Underwing Panel/ Hinge Box (14)
Slat Horn and Slat No. 0 (22)
Forward Flap Hinge Fairings (13)
Nose Assembly (11)/(2)-A3 Co-Production
Airstair (17)
Tires (6) and Wheels, Brakes (5)
Nose Gear Doors (1)-C19/(21) Co-Production
Avionics Access Door (1)-A3/(21) Co-Production
Main Landing Gear (15)
Nose Landing Gear (10)
Main Gear Doors Cargo Doors and Aft Service Door (1)-C19/(21) Co-Production

Following six years of negotiations between the parties, the agreement called initially for the purchase of 26 MD-80 twin-jet airliners, with 25 to be assembled in Shanghai. It was the first ever such agreement between a US aircraft manufacturer and the People's Republic of China. The pact also established a joint task force between the Long Beach Division of MDC and the Chinese aviation industry to carry out engineering and market feasibility studies aimed at cooperative development of new commercial transports in the future. It also provided for continuing efforts to expand export manufacturing trade and foreign industrial investments for China.

The first of 26 MD-80s was fully assembled at Long Beach and delivered to CAAC in December 1985. This was f/n 1093 s/n 49149, an MD-82 initially destined for Pacific Southwest Airlines as N948PS, but it was not taken up and was registered N1004S to MDC. It was delivered to CAAC on 12 December 1985 as B-2101, being transferred to China Eastern Airlines on

1 May 1988 and is still in service today. It joined two others and was followed by two more in December 1985.

The first sub-assemblies of aircraft components were shipped from Long Beach for CAAC in January 1986 and the first Shanghai-built aircraft rolled out of the Shanghai Aviation Industrial Corporation factory during early 1987. In the MD-80 production listing, f/n 1292/2 s/n 49501 to f/n 1746/25 s/n 49424 are all Shanghai built MD-82s, with the latter one being completed in January 1991. The production rate had shown a significant increase during the first half of 1989, but political turmoil in China and late deliveries of components from Long Beach slowed down the programme.

During April 1990, MDC and SAIC concluded an agreement to extend the co-production programme with an additional 10 airliners. This new order took the Shanghai assembly line into 1994, bringing total commitments to 40, of which 35 were built in China. As Chinese orders for twin-jet transports were

hotly contested, (with CAAC eventually ordering Boeing 737-200s and 737-300s), MDC at Long Beach had agreed in 1979 to have SAIC build undercarriage doors, access and service doors, door frames and even wing components. In July 1988, Long Beach awarded additional contracts covering the manufacture of complete MD-80 nose sections by the Chengdu Aircraft Corporation and of MD-80 horizontal stabilisers by SAIC, with Chinese-built components to be shipped to Long Beach.

The MD-80s in China are today operated by Shanghai-based China Eastern Airlines, which commenced service with the twin-jets in December 1983, and by China Northern Airlines, based in Shenyang, which began flying them in December 1985. Today China Eastern operates a large fleet which includes the MD-82, the DC-10 derived MD-11 and a successor to the MD-80, the MD-90-30. China Northern has also added the MD-90-30 to its large fleet.

ABOVE: The ramp scene at Long Beach in January 1987 with MD-80 models being prepared for airline delivery to Delta, Swissair, Continental, Minerva and Aero Lloyd. A decade later all but one of these operators would still be flying this popular airliner. The two Delta aircraft are MD-82s — N905DL, s/n 49536 f/n 1348, finished on 29 January 1987 and N904DL, s/n 49535 f/n 1347, which completed on 13 February 1987. In June 1988 N904DL was converted to MD-88 configuration. *Douglas*

ABOVE LEFT: Photo taken inside the MDC twin-jet paint booth in Building 87 at Long Beach. This unique building looks like a square with a triangle on top when viewed from above. Here the tail unit of a Delta Airlines MD-88 is receiving attention. *MDC*

The twin-jet airliners built in Shanghai are MD-82 models powered by two JT8D-217A engines rated at 20,000lb (88.8kN) take-off thrust. They seat 147 passengers in a mixed-class interior arrangement and have non-stop range of up to 2,360 statute miles (3,798km). Five MD-83s, incorporating auxiliary fuel tanks for extended range service, were also built as part of the programme.

The training of Chinese production managers and skilled workers for their jobs commenced in the summer of 1985. Large-scale exchange of personnel between China and the USA took place to accomplish the unique task. Furthermore, Long Beach personnel were assigned to work in China to provide a smooth manufacturing liaison.

TRUNKLINER

On 20 June 1992 an order was revealed for 20 MD-80s and 20 MD-90s for China Aero Technology Import & Export Corporation (CATIC) plus options for a further 130 MD-90s. On 25 June this received final government approval from Beijing. The agreement exceeded $1billion in value and provided for a growing demand for Chinese-assembled airliners in that nation's trunk and regional airline routes, but was sadly ill-fated.

The first three MD-80s delivered in 1995 were normal airliners, the remainder delivered in 1996 were quoted as MD-80Ts plus all the MD-90s will likewise be MD-90Ts. The 'T' stands for 'Trunkliner' the main difference being that these airliners have a new main landing gear with four wheels on each side, instead of the normal two-wheel arrangement. Assembly is with the Shanghai Aviation Industrial Corporation.

The first dual tandem undercarriage airliner is quoted as being SAIC No 35 used as a development aircraft. First production airliner MD-82T was quoted as SAIC No 39. MD-83 f/n 1872/29 s/n 53137 was the first to be marketed in the USA

by MDC after being ferried to Long Beach in June 1992. Today five Shanghai-built MD-83s are in service with TWA, these being N9401W f/n 1872/29 s/n 53137; N9402W f/n 1886/30 s/n 53138; N9403W f/n 1899/31 s/n 53139; N9404V f/n 1923/32 s/n 53140; and N9405T f/n 1935/33 s/n 53141. All were completed in China during 1992.

Long Beach forecast that MD-80/MD-90 Trunkliner production would commence in 1998 and continue past 2000, with production rates ranging from four to 10 airliners per year. The agreements called for a gradual increase in the level of component, fabrication and sub-assembly work in China's factories.

However, China's airlines have been buying Boeing 737s rather than MD-80s and MD-90s. During a state visit to the USA, Chinese president Jiang Zemin announced a $3billion order for 50 new Boeings, 35 of which are to be 737s.

Originally, 150 MD-90 airliners were to be built in China, but the programme proved to be a management and financial nightmare for Long Beach. 20 MD-90s are allotted to be built in Shanghai, together with another 20 built at Long Beach.

BELOW: Taken in early 1981, this photo shows MD-80s on the final assembly line at Long Beach. The first two are MD-81 N927PS for Pacific Southwest, completed on 9 October1980, and XA-AMA a DC-9-32 for Aero Mexico, completed 3 October 1980. The airliners were delivered to the respective airlines in January 1981. *MDC*

4 TECHNICAL SPECIFICATION

DC-9 ENGINE/TO WEIGHT PROGRESSION

Type	Powerplants	Thrust Rating	Max gross TO Weight	Notes
Series: D-9-10				
DC-9-11	JT8D-5	12,000lb (53.3kN)	77,000lb (34,926kg)	Fuselage length 104ft 5in (31.85m), wing span 89ft 5in (27.28m)
DC-9-12	JT8D-1 or -7	14,000lb (62.2kN)	85,700lb (38,873kg)	
DC-9-14	JT8D-5 or	12,000lb (53.3kN)	76,300lb (34,609kg)	
	JT8D1	14,000lb (62.2kN)		
DC-9-15	JT8D-1 or -7	14,000lb (62.2kN)	90,700lb (41,141kg)	
DC-9-15F (DC-9-15RC)	JT8D-7	14,000lb (62.2kN)	90,700lb (41,141kg)	RC; Rapid Change, palletized removable seats
DC-9-15F	JT8D-1	14,000lb (62.2kN)	90,700lb (41,141kg)	MC: Multiple change, folding removable seats
Series: DC-9-20				
DC-9-21	JT8D-9	14,500lb (64.4kN)	100,000lb (45,359kg)	High performance for high density altitude operations; fuselage 104ft 5in (31.85m), wing span 93ft 5in (28.5m)
	or JT8D-15	15,000lb (66.6kN)		
Series: DC-9-30				
DC-9-31	JT8D-1 or JT8D-7	14,000lb (62.2kN)	98,000lb (44,452kg)	Fuselage stretched to 119ft 5in (36.4m)
DC-9-32	JT8D-7	14,000lb (62.2kN)	108,000lb (48,988kg)	
	JT8D-9	14,500lb (64.4kN)		
	JT8D-11	15,000lb (66.6kN)		
	JT8D-15	15,500lb (66.6kN)		
DC-9-32F (AF)	JT8D-9 or JT8D-11	14,500lb (64.4kN) or	108,000lb (48,988kg)	All freighter configuration
DC-9-32CF	JT8D-9 or JT8D-11	15,000lb (66.6kN)	108,000lb (48,988kg)	Convertable freighter also offered as rapid change
DC-9-32 (C-9A)	JT8D-9	14,500lb (64.4k)		'Nightingale' military aeromedical version for USAF
DC-9-32	JT8D-9	14,500lb 64.4k)		'Skytrain II' logistics support for USN and US MC
DC-9-32 (VC-9C)	JT8D-9	14,500lb 64.4k)		Only three delivered to USAF. See msn 47668, 47670, 47671
DC-9-33F	JT8D-15	15,000lb (66.6kN)	114,000lb (51,709kg)	
DC-9-33CF	JT8D-9 or -11		114,000lb (51,709kg)	Convertable freighter also offered as rapid change
DC-9-34	JT8D-17	16,000lb (71.1kN)	121,000lb (54,884kg)	Extended range
DC-9-34CF	JT8D-17	16,000lb (71.1kN)	121,000lb (54,884kg)	
Series: DC-9-40				
DC-9-41	JT8D-11, or -15			Fuselage stretched to 125ft 7in (38.3m) high capacity, shorter range
Series DC-9-50				
DC-9-51	JT8D-17	16,000lb (71.1kN)	121,000lb (54,884kg)	Fuselage stretched to 133ft 7in (10.27m)
Series: DC-9-80 (MD-80)				
DC-9-81 (MD-81)	JT8D-209	18,500lb (82.2kN)	140,000lb (63,503kg)	Fuselage: 147ft 10in (44.8m), wing span 107ft 10in (32.6m)

Type	Powerplants Offered	Thrust Rating	Max gross TO Weight	Notes
DC-9-81 (MD-81)	JT8D-209	20,000lb (88.8kN)		
	217, 217A,-217C,-219	21,000lb (93.3kN)		
DC-9-82 (MD-82)	JT8D-217, -217A	20,000lb (88.8kN)		High performance for high density altitude operations, increased payload, range
DC-9-83 (MD-83)	JT8D-219	21,000lb (93.3kN)	160,000lb (72,574kg)	Increased range, reduced fuel consumption
DC-9-87 (MD-87)	JT8D-217C	20,000lb (88.8kN)	125,000lb (56,699kg)	Fuselage shortened to 119ft 1in (36.3m), taller tail, no rear doors, also certificated at higher MGTOWs
	JT8D-219	21,000lb (93.3kN)		
DC-9-88 (MD-88)	JT8D-219	20,000lb (88.8kN)	149,500lb (67.812kg)	Improved cockpits with EFIS, flight management systems; interior improvements
MD-90-30: IAE	V2525-D5	25,000lb (111kN)	156,000lb (70,760kg)	28,000lb (124.4kN) thrust on demand

MD-80 Series Vital Statistics

Overall length	147ft 11in (45.1m); **MD-87** 130.5ft (39.8m)
Width	107ft 10in (32.89m)
Height:	29ft 7in (9.02m)
Wing span	107ft 10in (32.87m)
Flight Crew	Two
Passengers	172 max; **MD-87** 139 max;
Range	1,580 to 2,750 statute miles (2,540 to 4,420km), depending on model.
Max take-off weight:	
MD-81	140,000lb (63,503kg)
MD-82 and basic MD-88	149,500lb (67,813kg)
MD-83 and MD-88	160,000lb (72,576kg)
MD-87	140,000lb (63,503kg)—— option 149,500lb (67,812kg)
Max cruise speed	575mph (925km/h)

MD-90 Vital Statistics

Overall length	152ft 7in (46.5m)
Wing span	107ft 10in (32.87m)
Cargo	1,300cu ft (36.8cu m)
Cruising speed	500mph (812km/h)
Passengers	152 (in mixed-class configuration)
Flight Crew	Two

Basic MD-90-30

Max take-off weight	156,000lb (70,760kg)
Max take-off weight option	160,500lb (72,800kg)
Range	2,400 statute miles

Higher Gross Weight MD-90-30

Max take-off weight	168,000lb (76,203kg)
Range	2,510 statute miles (4,040km)
Range option	2,765 statute miles (4,450km) with auxiliary tank
Take-off thrust	25,000lb-28,000lb option (11,340kg-12,700kg option)
Min runway length	5,000ft (1,524m) on 550 statute-mile (885km) operation with full passenger load
Min runway length	7,450ft (2,270m) at max take-off weight

POWER FOR THE MD SERIES

Located at East Hartford, Connecticut, USA, Pratt & Whitney Aircraft was formed in 1925. Today as part of the huge United Technologies Corporation, the Pratt & Whitney Group is the world's largest producer of gas turbine engines. Excluding Pratt & Whitney Canada, it had by 1989 delivered over 70,000 aircraft gas turbines, including more than 25,000 airline jet engines.

It can be revealed that the development of a re-fanned JT8D was initially sponsored by the US National Aeronautic & Space Administration, NASA. By combining the high-pressure compressor, HP turbine spool, and combustion section of the proven JT8D-9 engine with a new six-stage low pressure compressor and LP turbine, and adding a new bypass duct, Pratt & Whitney was able to develop the JT9D-200 series. Compared with earlier JT8D versions, the new series offered increased thrust as well as substantial reductions in noise and specific fuel consumption. Engine length and diameter were increased respectively from 120 to 150in (3.05 to 3.81m) and from 42.5 to 56.34in (1.08 to 1.43m). This still enabled re-fanned JT8Ds to be installed in nacelles not significantly larger than those of earlier JT8D versions.

The earlier successful JT8D-9 was no stranger to Long Beach production lines having, along with the JTD8-9A, powered the Douglas DC-9-20, -30, -40, and the military C-9A, C-9B and VC-9C transports.

A pair of JT8D-109s re-fanned prototypes were also fitted to a DC-9-32 (s/n 47649 f/n 741) under a NASA contract, and the combination first flew on 9 January 1975. After being re-engined with the JT8D-11s specified for installation in the DC-9-20, -30 and -40, the airliner was delivered as DC-9-31 (YU-AJR) to Inex Adria Airways on 5 March 1975. On 10 September 1976 it was destroyed in a mid-air collision with Trident 3B G-AWZT, near Vrolec village, north-east of Zagreb, Yugoslavia.

Even prior to the pressure from the keenest prospective customer, Swissair, being able to obtain a production commitment from Long Beach, the stretched and re-engined twin-jet was the subject of several proposed new configurations. Examples being DC-9-RSS — a Re-fanned-Stretch-Stretch; DC-9-55

RIGHT: One of the most powerful additions to the Pratt & Whitney JT8D gas turbine family is the 're-fanned' JT8D-200 series which powered the early MD-80 airliners. It traces its beginnings to NASA's 'Quiet Engine' programme which was conducted between 1972–1975. The JT8D-209 engine entered commercial service on the Swissair MD-81 which flew its first service on 5 October 1980. *Pratt & Whitney*

BELOW RIGHT: Receiving attention on the Long Beach ramp is f/n 909 s/n 48000 later registered N980DC — the very first MD-80. It is painted in the MDC corporate livery and was called DC-9 Super 80. This photo was taken prior to its first flight and no registration has yet been painted on the engine nacelles. Later it was repainted in the MDC purple and gold livery and renamed MD-80. It was referred to as '909' remaining in the experimental category for its complete, illustrious career. It is currently in storage at Grayson County Airport, Sherman, Texas. *MDC*

BELOW Engineers at the Pratt & Whitney plant located at Hartford, Connecticut prepare another JT8D-200 series turbofan for delivery. An exclusive engine for the MD-80 series airliner, the JT8D-200 covers the 18,500-22,000lb (82.1kN-98kN) thrust range. The JT8D-200 powered MD-80 airliners meet current environmental regulations for noise and emissions. Since commencing revenue service in 1980 over 2,600 engines have been produced in five different models, logging over 45 million hours of operation. *Pratt & Whitney*

JT8D-200 SERIES TURBOFAN

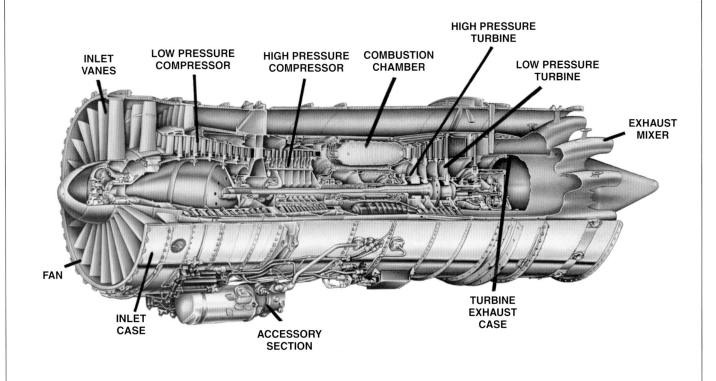

and DC-9-SC fitted with a new super-critical wing etc. At this time the company even considered the joint development with Dassault-Breguet of the ASMR (Advanced Short-to-Medium Range) derivative of the French designed Mercure. Research soon proved that a new version of the ubiquitous DC-9 would prove less costly to develop and manufacture than the French ASMR and, as it would reduce training, spares and facility requirements, was clearly far more attractive to the many existing DC-9 operators.

THE JT8D-200 SERIES

The reduced noise derivative of the JT8D combines the HP compressor, HP turbine spool and combustion section of the JT8D-9 with advanced LP technology. It offers increased thrust with reduced noise and specific fuel consumption. The fan has increased diameter. The new six-stage LP compressor, integral with the fan, offers increased pressure ratio. The LP turbine has 20 percent greater annular area and achieves a higher efficiency. Surrounding the engine is a new bypass duct. The exhaust system includes a 12 lobe mixer. Certification of the JT8D-209 was awarded by the Federal Aviation Administration (FAA) in June 1979.

Current models of the 200 series include the following:

JT8D-209	18,000lb st (82.2kN) rating to 25°; 19,250lb st (85.6kN) in case of loss of thrust on any other engine. First service October 1980 on the MD-81.
JT8D-217	20,000lb st (88.96kN); 20,850lb st (92.75kN) after loss of thrust on any other engine
JT8D-217A	Take-off thrust to 28.9° up to 5,000ft (1,525m)
JT8D-217C	Incorporates JT8D-219 performance improvements
JT8D-219	Rated at 21,000lb st (93.4kN) with a reserve power of 21,7000lb st (96,5kN)

STOL

In 1978 an attempt at meeting short take off and landing requirements (STOL) in Japan had been made with the DC-9 Super 80SF, combining the advanced wing and engines of the basic Super 80 with the fuselage of the DC-9-40. Most of the development costs would have been covered under the Super 80 programme. However, it was decided that the progressive installation of the more powerful JT8D-217 engines in the versions already projected would provide similar airfield performance and so the Super 80SF was not proceeded with.

Prior to the first flight of the DC-9-50 in December 1974 Long Beach had turned its attention to the next major development — known as the DC-9-60 — to take advantage of the new re-fanned versions of the successful Pratt & Whitney JT8D engine. An early example of this engine, the JT8D-109, was flight-tested on DC-9-32 N54638 commencing on 9 January 1975. In close cooperation with Pratt & Whitney, a

number of advanced studies explored a number of other DC-9 derivatives, ranging from the odd-ball designated DC-9-17R powered by JT8D-17R turbofans incorporating automatic power reserve, to re-fanned versions such as the DC-9-50RS (Re-fan Stretched) DC-9-50RSS (Re-fan, Super Stretch) and the later and similar DC-9-55.

All these had a bigger wing, more power and a stretched fuselage, which would have enabled the new aircraft to carry more passengers than the proposed DC-9-50 over the same distance as the extended-range DC-9-34. Another innovative proposal already mentioned was the DC-9-SC, which featured an all new super-critical wing. Actively under consideration was the DC-9-QSF (Quiet Short Field) offered to the Japanese airlines who were seeking a replacement for their NAMC YS-11 turboprop airliner.

This was basically a DC-9-40 with a new wing which was enlarged by the insertion of a 10ft (3.04m) centre section, and re-fanned JT8D-209 engines, rated at 18,000lb st (80kN). With a gross weight of 114,000lb (51,710kg) the DC-9-QSF was intended to carry a passenger load of 120, all the year round, from 4,000ft (1,200m) runways.

Similar claims to meet the requirements of the Japanese airlines were made for the proposed DC-9-22, first announced in 1977. This up-rated development of the DC-9-21, the 'hot-rod' airliner operated by the Scandinavian Airlines Systems (SAS), which featured the installation of the more powerful JT8D-15 or -17 turbofans, additional wing spoilers and an improved braking system. Both these designs were eventually shelved in favour of the more advanced concepts, this clearly and almost exclusively pointed the way to the new re-fanned JT8D-200 series of turbofans, which was given the go-ahead in March 1977. Because of the high costs involved uprated engines were rejected — plus on grounds of noise. New engines were also costly. The all new super-critical wing was also discarded as being too expensive.

INTERNATIONAL AERO ENGINES

With all the speculation as to whether there would ever be a merger between two of the big three aerospace engine manufacturers, it must be recalled that collaboration between three took place some decades ago. Possibly the most successful current collaboration commenced way back in 1983 with the formation of International Aero Engines (IAE) in which both Rolls-Royce and Pratt & Whitney have a stake and are in fact lead partners.

The venture's success is even more remarkable when one considers that originally there were five collaborators, the others being Motoren-Und Turbinen (MTU) Daimler Benz of Germany, FiatAvio from Italy, and a group of Japanese companies, Mitsubishi, Kawasaki and Ishikawajima-Harima, operating under the title of the Japanese Aero Engines Corporation (JAEC). In 1966 FiatAvio sold its share, so the unique make-up of IAE is Pratt & Whitney and Rolls-Royce 32.5 percent, JAEC 23 percent and MTU Daimler Benz 12 percent.

The consortium set up home in an old schoolhouse in East Hartford, Connecticut. Today its American base is inside the Pratt & Whitney complex just a few hundred metres from that

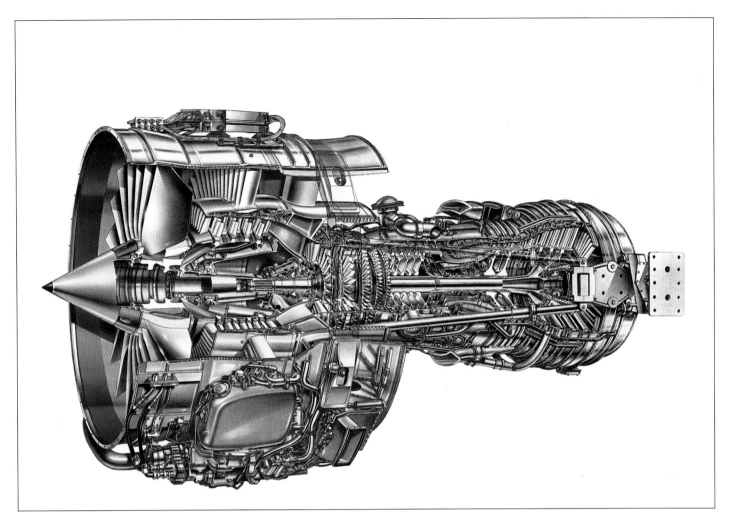

ABOVE: International Aero Engines (IAE) — a consortium with Rolls-Royce and Pratt & Whitney as the leading partners — build the V2500-D5 for the MD-90.
IAE

original location. Some business pundits would inevitably agree that bringing together international partners to work in a highly complex collaboration is just about the most risky option available. But in fact that is exactly how the new V2500 aero engine was born.

In 1989 the first V2500 engine from IAE entered service, and by August 1997 this engine series had just passed five million flying hours. Since 1989 a family of engines under the V2500 designation has been developed. The MDC MD-90 twin-jet airliner utilises two of eight thrust ratings, the V2525-D5 and V-2528-D5. The order book for the V2500 stood at over 2,000 engines by August 1997, with a total value of over $13billion. The customer base is made up of over 70 airlines and leasing companies with the MD-90 having customers in Europe, Asia, the Middle East and North America.

Though IAE does not have its own engine shops, there are eight locations around the world for major work plus nearly 300 representatives, the after-sales service support benefiting from the existing Rolls-Royce and Pratt & Whitney networks.

To find a name, IAE combined the Roman 'V' representing the five original partners, and the number 2500, an abbreviation of the engine's maximum thrust of 25,000lb (111kN) —

the equivalent of 12.5 tons of power. Each of the partner companies involved was given responsibility for developing and delivering one of the five engine sections or modules. JAEC controlled the fan and low pressure compressor, Rolls-Royce took responsibility for the high pressure compressor, Pratt & Whitney had the task of producing the combustor and high pressure turbine, while MTU the low pressure turbine and FiatAvio the gearbox.

The V2500 engines are manufactured on both sides of the Atlantic. The engines destined for Airbus Industries in France are assembled by Rolls-Royce in Derby, while those for MDC are shipped to Long Beach by Pratt & Whitney from East Hartford.

One of the most noticeable features of a jet engine is its fan blades, and in the case of the V2500, they provide a good example of the advanced but proven technology contributed by the IAE partners. The V2500 uses unique hollow blades designed and developed by Rolls-Royce. These are made from two sheets of titanium which are heated to a state where they can be moulded. While they are being twisted into their final aerodynamic shape the two halves are bonded together, then gas is blown between the sheets, producing a metal honeycomb centre. The resulting semi-hollow blade is light yet extremely strong and has the ability to bend on impact, a vital asset which dramatically reduces the potential damage from objects such as runway debris and birds.

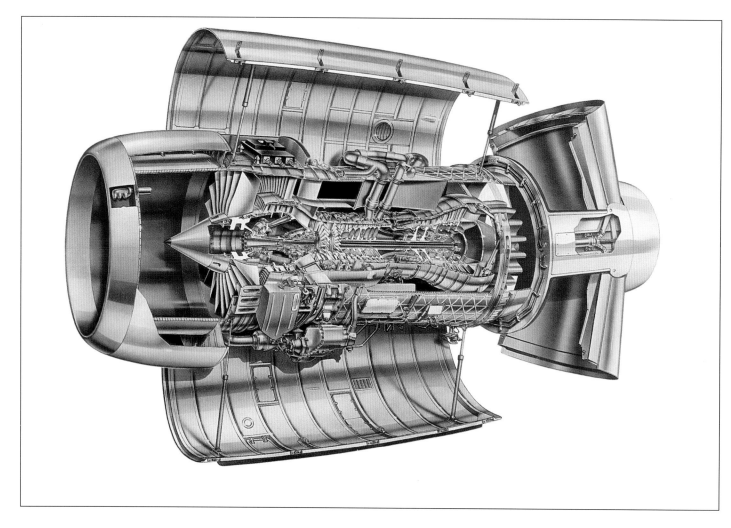

NOISE-LEVEL COMPARISONS
FAR PART 36, STAGE 3 CONDITIONS

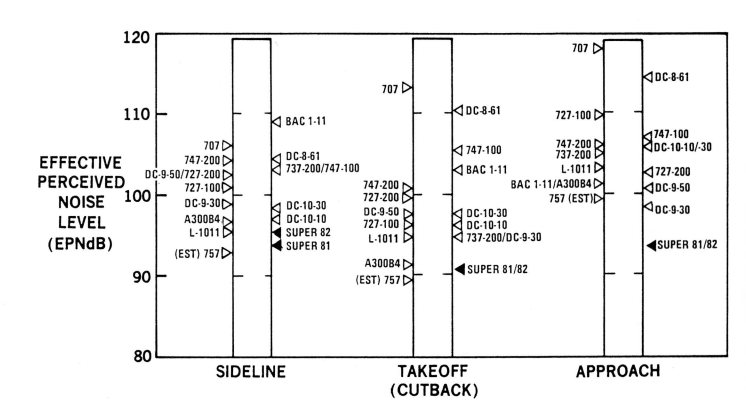

Pratt & Whitney's 'floatwall' combustor is another piece of V2500 technology in which, as its name implies, the unit has twin walls, the outer skin separated from the metal closest to the centre of the burner by a gap which allows it to remain cool and less susceptible to the type of cracking experienced by conventional designs.

The engine's low noise signature is good news for both passengers and airport communities. The V2500-powered MD-90 for instance, is up to 25 decibels below today's statutory limits and well inside any proposed noise limitations. This outstanding 'green' advantage comes from detailed attention to design. The V2500's full length cowl acts as a barrier to side noise. A positive benefit is also gained by mixing cold air flow from the bypass with the hot jetstream. Furthermore the profile of the wide-chord fan blades also contributes to noise reduction, just as it protects the engine from foreign object damage (FOD).

The V2500 also provides airlines with yet another important technical benefit — commonality. Apart from the way the engine is mounted on the airliner, all versions of the V2500 are mechanically identical. Any change in thrust is simply commanded by computer. With over 70 airline and leasing company customers around the world, plus orders to power almost 800 aircraft and a $12billion order book, the V2500 continues to prove that conventions can be successfully broken down in the world of international business.

BMW ROLLS-ROYCE BR715

BMW Rolls-Royce reached another milestone on 28 April 1997 with the successful first run of the BR715, the powerplant for the new MD-95 airliner, at the company's development and assembly centre located at Dahlewitz, near Berlin, Germany. Designed for 22,000lb (98kN) thrust the engine has been certificated at 21,000lb (93kN) thrust and within 24 hours of its first run, it achieved 25,745lb (110kN) thrust, albeit on a cold morning.

The BR715 turbofan has been developed for 90-130 seater regional aircraft and has been selected as the sole powerplant for the MD-95-30 twin-jet airliner. First flight was scheduled from Long Beach for the second quarter of 1998 followed by Federal Aviation Administration (FAA) certification and entry into service with AirTran who as ValuJet was the launch customer. (ValuJet was re-named AirTran in August 1997.) There is great confidence that Boeing with their take-over at MDC Long Beach will support the MD-95 programme as it has no competition, while the Long Beach designers are looking at smaller versions of the airliner.

Second in the BMW Rolls-Royce BR700 family of clean, quiet, fuel and cost efficient engines for the next century, the BR715 engine family was launched in March 1991 with a thrust range of 14,000-23,000lb (62.2kN-102.4kN) and is

based on a single core. This has a 10-stage high-pressure turbine. The engine has a 58in (1.47m) fan chamber and is based on the BR700 core with the high pressure compressor improved for mass flow and efficiency and the high pressure turbine enhanced for increased durability using single crystal turbine blade material.

The innovative design of the BR715 high by-pass ratio turbofan engine includes the largest ever 'blisk' (combined blade and disk) used in a civil engine, an intermediate case which is the largest single piece of titanium casting in a civil engine, and the very first incorporation of design aspects from the Rolls-Royce advanced low pressure system research into a production engine programme.

Early tests on the first development BR715 engine will include a performance assessment with fan and low pressure turbine strain gauging. The engine will undergo crosswind testing and thrust reverse cycling at the Rolls-Royce facility located at Hucknall in the United Kingdom. The length of the BR715 engine is 19ft (5.90m), fan diameter 58in (1.47m) and weight including the nacelle is 6,155lb (2,792kg).

Early in 1998, BMW Rolls-Royce delivered the first two BR715s to Boeing's Douglas Products Division at Long Beach ready for the first flight of the MD-95, then predicted in the second quarter of the year.

ULTRA-HIGH-BYPASS ENGINES

With a look into the future, the MDC design and engineering team trained its conceptual thoughts for further development of its twin-jet airliner series during the mid-1980s. Among the resulting designs were more than one known as MD-90, before that designation was eventually applied to a production series airliner.

The 'drawing board' computer activities of the Long Beach team produced what was tentatively referred to as the MD-X during 1985. It was designed firmly around the new concept of Ultra-High-Bypass (UHB) engines driving highly-contoured, counter-rotating, multi-blade fans. Developing the UHB engine, which was also referred to as Unducted Fan (UDF), for the basis of a new range of airliner derivatives was undertaken in cooperation with Aeritalia, Saab-Scania and Science Applications International Corporation of San Diego.

The project crystallised into two new variants of the successful Long Beach built twin-jet airliner, the 114-seat MD-91X and the 165-seat MD-92X, which were being offered to potential customer airlines from early 1988. Whereas propfan engines could be substituted for the rear-mounted Pratt & Whitney JT8D-217 turbo fans on its MD-80 Series, neither Airbus Industries or Boeing could do so with their A320 Series or Boeing 737/757/767/777 Series due to their wing-mounted engines.

In the four years from 1985, MDC promoted UHB engines as the power-plants for new short-to-medium-range airliners, with propfan-power claimed to yield 25 to 35 percent fuel savings over state-of-the-art turbofans, and 50 percent saving compared with the MD-80.

Flight testing from Edwards Air Force Base started on 18

ABOVE LEFT: **BMW Rolls-Royce is providing the powerplant for the new MD-95 airliner — the BR715.** *BMW Rolls-Royce*

LEFT: Engine noise levels are very important factors in today's competitive marketplace. This MDC-prepared chart shows the relative positions of the competition when the **MD-81 and MD-82 entered the market.** *MDC*

May 1987, using General Electric GE36 Unducted Fan engines on the port side of the MD-80 prototype N980DC, f/n 909 s/n 48000. This was used to demonstrate the potential of a proposed re-engined MD-88 and propfan powered MD-90 series. Initially the GE engines were tested with two 8-blade fans of 12ft (3.66m) diameter. On 15 August flight test trials with an improved engine with a 10in blade fan in front and an 8-blade fan at the rear commenced. Tests with a Pratt & Whitney-Allison 578-DX powerplant commenced in March 1989, the first flight taking place at Edwards on 13 April 1989.

The UHB demonstrator was modified to test the 20,000lb (88.8kN) thrust 578-DX propfan engine jointly developed by Allison and Pratt & Whitney. It drove two sets of 6-bladed counter-rotating propfans and was again mounted in the port nacelle. However, by this time, MDC was about to concede that the development of propfan-powered airliners was not yet justified.

MDC also entered a propfan-powered MD-87 in the US Navy's Long Range ASW Capable Aircraft (LRAACA) competition, but the Lockheed P-7, a development of the P-3 Orion, was given preference.

Yet a further MDC project was an all-new propfan follow-on to the MD-80, known as the MD-94X. In addition to the UHB engine, this 160-180 passenger airliner featured laminar and turbulent boundary layer control, very high aspect ratio super-critical wings, flight-critical active stability augmentation digital control systems, fly-by-wire and fly-by-light technologies and all-electric secondary power systems. A UHB retrofit programme for the MD-80 was also on the drawing board, said to achieve an up to 40 percent reduction in fuel consumption.

The MDC design and engineering team had not been idle: the company was also able to present to the airlines another alternative, the MD-96V series powered by the successfully developed International Aero Engine (IAE) V2500 advanced high-bypass engine. The series initially comprised the similar-sized MD-91V with accommodation for 114 passengers, and the larger 165-seat MD-92V. Then, in response to airline interest a still larger third variant was added to the programme. This was the MD-93V fitted out in a two-class configuration with up to 180 seats.

The new designs became finely tuned towards optimum customer requirements, and it soon became evident that the immediate future lay with the new V2500, a fully developed and certified engine. This offered a considerable advantage in a highly competitive business.

Mention must be made of the proposed MD-90-30ER (Extended Range) military C9D Skytrain III transport for the US Navy who had boasted about the great efficiency of their fleet of Skytrain III transports, mainly DC-9-30 variants. Powered by two fuel-efficient V2518-D5 engines, each producing 28,000lb (124.3kN) of thrust MDC believe the result is a highly-reliable transport stepping into the 21st century as the pro-environment aviation leader.

The interior of the C-9D is configured as a COMBI (Combined Cargo and/or Passenger) aircraft. In the combi interior there are up to four cargo pallet positions forward with up to 69 passenger seats, aft galleys, lavatories, overhead bag racks and storage cabinets. In the all-passenger mode, the C-9D can accommodate up to 124 passengers, with the existing forward galleys and lavatories.

Currently, the proposed C-9D is being studied for incorporating a main instrument panel with six across, 8-in Liquid Crystal Displays (LCD) panels. In addition to the baseline MD-90 avionics option will include Global Position System (GPS), Satellite (SATCOM), and dual UHF communications. Wing span is 107ft 10in (32.87m), length 152ft 7in (46.54m).

During the early 1990s, in order to provide a smoother transition to the new MD-90, MDC was considering an improved version incorporating some of the best elements of the MD-90 series design with a new engine for the existing MD-80 airframe. In addition to the engine, (which existed only on paper) the MD-80 Advanced was to offer a new flight deck instrumentation package and a completely new passenger compartment design. All would be available in retrofit for existing MD-80s and was forecast to be in service by July 1993. Development of the MD-80 Advanced was dependent on whether Pratt & Whitney launched the JT8D-290, an improved version of the successful JT8D-217C, with a lower noise signature and a 25 percent target reduction in noxious emissions.

The MD-80 Advanced was to incorporate the advanced flight deck from the MD-88, including a choice of reference systems, with an inertial reference system as standard fitting and optional attitude-heading equipment. It was to be equipped with an electronic flight instrument system, an optional second flight management system computer, light emitting diode dot matrix electronic engine and system displays. A Honeywell windshear computer and provision for an optional traffic-alert and collision avoidance system were also to be included. A new interior would have a 12 percent increase in overhead baggage space and stowage compartment lights that come on when the door opens, as well as a new video system featuring drop-down liquid crystal display monitors above

WHEN IS A DC-9 AN MD-80 ?

The rather perplexed question 'when is a Douglas DC-9 a McDonnell Douglas MD-80?' is often asked. This arises more especially if an operator decides to decorate its airliner ident with an anomaly which confuses the issue. A few examples are: the inscription 'DC-9 Super 80' on the engines of the MD-82 PH-MBY, f/n 1005 s/n 48048; Austral's MD-81 which had 'DC-9' inscribed on top of the fuselage, this being N87714Q f/n 948 s/n 48024; and the PSA MD-81 N982PS, f/n 974 s/n 48052, which had 'DC-9' on the engine nacelles.

As the MD-80 was not in effect a new aircraft, it continued to be operated under an amendment to the original DC-9 Type Certificate, issued in the USA by the Federal Aviation Agency (FAA) which certificates the airworthiness of a particular type. This data sheet 'prescribes conditions and limitations under which the product for which the Type Certificate was issued meets the airworthiness requirement of the Civil Air Regulations.'

A Type Certificate is issued with the aircraft model designa-

ABOVE: The image of a newly delivered Alaska Airlines MD-80 is reflected on a wet flight ramp at Long Beach on 23 March 1992 when the airline took delivery of MD-83 N940AS, the 1,000th MD-80 series twin-jet. The Seattle-based airline currently operates a fleet of nearly 50 of the MD-80 series aircraft, serving in excess of 38 cities. The photo shows well the nosewheel assembly, and gives an idea of the size of the aircraft — it's 147ft 10in (45.06m) long and 30ft 2in (9.19m) high.
A P Publications

RIGHT: The UHB demonstrator N980DC was modified to flight test the 20,000lb (88.8kN) thrust 578-DX propfan engine, jointly developed by Pratt & Whitney and Allison. It had two sets of six-bladed counter-rotating propfans. First flight was made from Edwards AFB on 13 April 1989. The DAC conceded that the development of propfan powered airliners was not yet justified, and further test work was ended in mid-1989. *Douglas*

tion exactly as it appears on the manufacturer's application, including use of hyphens or decimal points, and should match what is stamped on the aircraft's data or name plate. What the manufacturer chooses to call an aircraft for marketing or promotional purposes is irrelevant to the airworthiness authorities.

The amendment covering the first variant in the series, the DC-9-81, was approved on 26 August 1980. All models have since been approved under additional amendments to the DC-9 Type Certificate.

In 1983, MDC decided that the DC-9-80 (Super 80) would be designated the MD-80. While MDC has kept separate records for DC-9s and MD-80s, the MD-80 is a stretched version of the earlier successful DC-9, but with re-fanned engines and modernised avionics.

However, instead of merely using the MD- prefix as a marketing symbol, an application was made to again amend the Type Certificate to include the MD-81, MD-82 and MD-83. This change was dated 10 March 1986, and the Type Certificate declared that although the MD designator could be used in parentheses, it must be accompanied by the official designation, for example DC-9-81 (MD-81). All Long Beach airliners in the MD-80 series thereafter had MD-81, MD-82 or MD-83 stamped on the name plate.

Although not certificated until 21 October 1987, MDC had already applied for models DC-9-87 and DC-9-87F on 13 February 1985. This derivative was similarly officially designated DC-9-87 (MD-87), although no name plates were stamped DC-9-87. The DC-9-87F was waiting to be certificated. For the MD-88, an application for a Type Certificate model amendment was made after the earlier changes, so there never was a DC-9-88, only the MD-88, which was certificated on 10 December 1987.

Another quirk of MDC nomenclature was the use of a hyphen in the MD-90 designation when discussing the airliner series, but without a hyphen between 'MD' and '90' when referring to a specific model (as in MD90-30).

One final interesting point is that there was a DC-9 series 60, an earlier proposal for an airliner which was to have been powered by '20-tonne' French CFM International CFM56 or Pratt & Whitney JT10D engines. So the version announced in October 1977 should perhaps have been designated DC-9 Series 70 (DC-9-70): but, as it was scheduled to enter service in 1980, the opportunity presented itself for marketing it as the Series 80 or Super 80 for the 'eighties'.

One solution to the problem of Long Beach twin-jet nomenclature which may not be entirely welcome to MDC fans is the Boeing Commercial Airplane Group decision to designate the new MD-95 as the Boeing 717-200.

COCKPIT

The MD-80 cockpit was the most advanced of its time. Long Beach design engineers, working closely with the Super 80 project pilot 'Knick' Knickerbocker, developed a cockpit configuration which ensured maximum operational efficiency with a minimum total crew workload level. Taking full advantage of digital technology and its inherent potential for integration of systems, they were able to redesign an already efficient cockpit and improve it in many ways.

The MD-80 was meant to be operated by two pilots, and first operations in the United States by PSA were with two pilots as certificated. But PSA's crews were not union members. Two-pilot crewing was not to the liking of ALPA (the US Airline Pilots' Association), though it was normal in the MD-80's forerunner, the DC-9.

The union's position was a real threat to the future of the airliner. A third flight-deck crew member was eventually ruled unnecessary on safety grounds by a Presidential task force, but only after Southern Airways had pulled out of an order for the MD-80, and many other established Douglas customers had avoided MD-80 orders, because of the potential cost of three-person crews.

TRANSITION TO MD-90

Roswell Industrial Air Center, an ex-USAF air base located in New Mexico, with an elevation of 3,670ft (1,119m) above mean sea level, suffering from high temperatures, is used frequently by the Long Beach Flight Test Division for checking out new pilots and continuation training flights with the MD-80, MD-90 and MD-11 airliners. Transition to type usually follows a day in the flight simulator located at Long Beach. The MDC policy is to offer MD-90 operators better performance and lower noise levels than its predecessor the MD-80, while retaining a common pilot type rating with the many earlier DC-9 derivatives. This policy inevitably limited the changes that the Long Beach design engineers could incorporate into the MD-90, especially in the cockpit.

Airline pilots accustomed to flying the Boeing 757/767 or Airbus A320/340 airliners find the MD-90 cockpit a throwback to earlier aircraft that did not include large electronic displays and highly automated systems. However, pilots familiar

ABOVE RIGHT: The MD-80 nomenclature refers to the whole family of MD-80 models that started with the MD-81. This flew first on 18 October 1979 and was sold with JT8D-209 engines and seating for about 135 passengers. Swissair, along with Austrian Airlines, became the launch customer when it ordered 15 plus five options in October 1977. The first Swissair MD-81 service took place on 5 October 1980 operating a Zurich–Frankfurt round trip. By July 1997 Swissair was still operating seven MD-81s. Here is HB-INY which was completed on 24 February 1988, delivered on 25 March and named *Basserdorf*. *Chris Dogget*

CENTRE RIGHT: The MD-82 flew first on 8 January 1981, powered by higher thrust JT8D217s allowing improved payload and range or the ability to fly in 'hot and high' conditions. Here is B-2107, the second MD-80 to be assembled in China, delivered to China Eastern Airlines on 17 December 1987 from the Shanghai factory. China Eastern Airlines is based at Shanghai Hongqiao International Airport in the People's Republic of China and received its first MD-82, B-2101, on 1 May 1988. By May 1997 the airline was operating a fleet of 13 MD-82s. *MDC*

RIGHT: The MD-83 offered improved power in the shape of JT8D219s, carried more fuel and saw an improvement in range. The extra fuel was located in two extra fuel tanks just aft of the centre section; the extra weight required modifications to the undercarriage, floor and wings. It first flew on 17 December 1984 and saw service first with Alaska Airlines in February 1985 (see photo on page 37). This photo shows MD-83 TC-INC *Ersel* leased from Irish Aerospace on 3 April 1995 by Sunways Intersun Havacilik. Until its sudden collapse late in 1997 Sunway was an international charter passenger and cargo operator based in Antalya, Turkey. *Mark Nutter*

with the successful DC-9 series, feel comfortable in the MD-90 cockpit. The MDC designers, with the influence of company and airline pilots, did improve the visibility from the cockpit, reduce clutter on the instrument panel, and make sensible changes to the aircraft's system displays and controls.

Major changes are naturally not evident from the cockpit, but do extend the life to a family of twin-jet airliners that started with the DC-9-10 in 1965. The most significant change in the MD-90 is the replacement of the 21,000lb-thrust (93.3kN) Pratt & Whitney P&W JT8D engines used in the MD-80 with International Aero Engine (IAE) V2500 series engines. This has a 25,000lb-thrust (111kN) rating, with a 28,000lb (124.3kN) optional. The new engine gives the noise levels well below Stage 3 requirements and even below potential Stage 4 levels. The V2500 engine also emits lower amounts of carbon monoxide, oxides of nitrogen and hydrocarbons.

Other improvements in the MD-90 include the installation of a new passenger interior and vacuum lavatories. A 4.75ft (1.4m) plug added to the standard MD-83 fuselage allows the new airliner to fly with a mixed class seating of 158 passengers, or a maximum of 172 seats. The additional length accentuates the comparatively small wings of the MD-90. They are essentially the same as those on the earlier DC-9 with added strength. The wing size also partially explains the maximum 37,000ft (11,278m) certificated altitude for the MD-90.

As is already well known, the Long Beach built transports have a fine reputation for durability and long life, which explains why there are still more than the 2,000 DC-9 and MD-80 airliners still in service. The design service life of the DC-9 was 30,000 hours and 40,000 landings, and for the MD-83 was 50,000 hours and landings. The design service life for the MD-90 is for 90,000 hours and 60,000 landings. The combination of durability, excellent performance, cabin flexibility and quietness inherent in the MD-90 make it an excellent airliner for operators.

ABOVE RIGHT: The MD-87 is a shortened version of the MD-80. Its length of 130ft 5in (39.75m) is 17ft 5in (5.3m) shorter and it is notable for having the first EFIS cockpit of the MD-80 family. Powered by JT8D217Cs, it has a tapered low drag tail cone and an increased height tail fin (modifications that are retro-fitted to later-model MD-80s). The MD-87 first flew on 4 December 1986 six years after Austrian, along with Swissair and Southern Airways, had become the third launch customer for the MD-87 when it was announced on 19 October 1977, placing firm orders for eight plus four options. Today the Vienna-based airline operates five MD-81s, five MD-82s, two MD-83s and five MD-87s. Depicted is MD-87 OE-LML *Salzburg*, which was completed on 14 November 1987 and delivered on 23 December. By the end of December 1997 it had flown 26,801 hours and accomplished 15,556 landings. *Chris Doggett*

RIGHT: The MD-88 answered an order for 80 aircraft by Delta in 1986. It first flew on 15 August 1987 and entered service in January 1988. It is similar to the MD-82 — indeed, the first eight aircraft delivered to Delta were just up-engined and modified MD-82s — but with an EFIS cockpit, which includes flight management and inertial reference systems, more composite materials used in its airframe and a redesigned interior which usually seats about 135 passengers. Midway Airlines is based in Chicago and at one time it had a fleet of 120-seat MD-87s, two MD-88s, three MD-83s and four MD-82s all three seating 143-passengers. All had eight first class seats. This is MD-87 N8808ML completed in December 1989 and delivered on 10 January 1990. *Chris Doggett*

SUPER 80 FLIGHT COMPARTMENT CONFIGURATION
STANDARD (DS/8000)

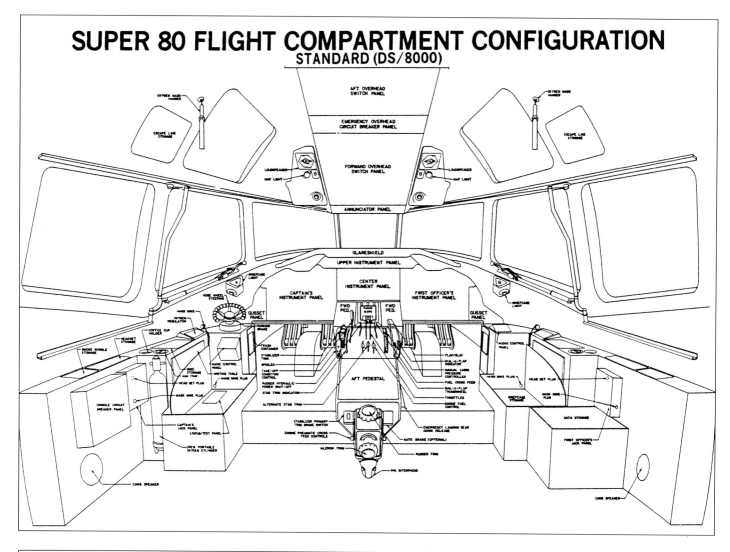

GENERAL CHARACTERISTICS

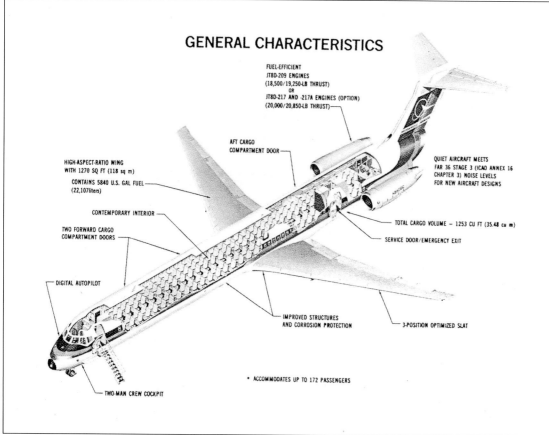

FUEL-EFFICIENT
JT8D-209 ENGINES
(18,500/19,250-LB THRUST)
OR
JT8D-217 AND -217A ENGINES (OPTION)
(20,000/20,850-LB THRUST)

AFT CARGO
COMPARTMENT DOOR

QUIET AIRCRAFT MEETS
FAR 36 STAGE 3 (ICAO ANNEX 16
CHAPTER 3) NOISE LEVELS
FOR NEW AIRCRAFT DESIGNS

HIGH-ASPECT-RATIO WING
WITH 1270 SQ FT (118 sq m)

CONTAINS 5840 U.S. GAL FUEL
(22,107liters)

CONTEMPORARY INTERIOR

TWO FORWARD CARGO
COMPARTMENT DOORS

DIGITAL AUTOPILOT

TOTAL CARGO VOLUME - 1253 CU FT (35.48 cu m)

SERVICE DOOR/EMERGENCY EXIT

IMPROVED STRUCTURES
AND CORROSION PROTECTION

3-POSITION OPTIMIZED SLAT

* ACCOMMODATES UP TO 172 PASSENGERS

TWO-MAN CREW COCKPIT

ABOVE: Flight compartment configuration of the 'Super 80'. Note the two-man crewing arrangement, today so widespread but unusual in the late 1970s/early 1980s. *MDC*

LEFT: MDC artwork highlighting the MD-80's general characteristics. *MDC*

ABOVE RIGHT: General arrangement drawing of the family showing graphically the shortened MD-87. *MDC*

RIGHT: Air California operated the MD-80 during 1981 prior to a merger with American Airlines and was involved in a thorough passenger survey. Although a majority rated all interiors as attractive, the sleek contour and interior features of the MD-80, as seen in this photo, were rated 'very attractive' far more often than those of the Boeing 737 and 727. The MD-80's greater space per passenger resulted in higher comfort ratings. *MDC*

MD-81/-82/-83/-87/-88
GENERAL ARRANGEMENT

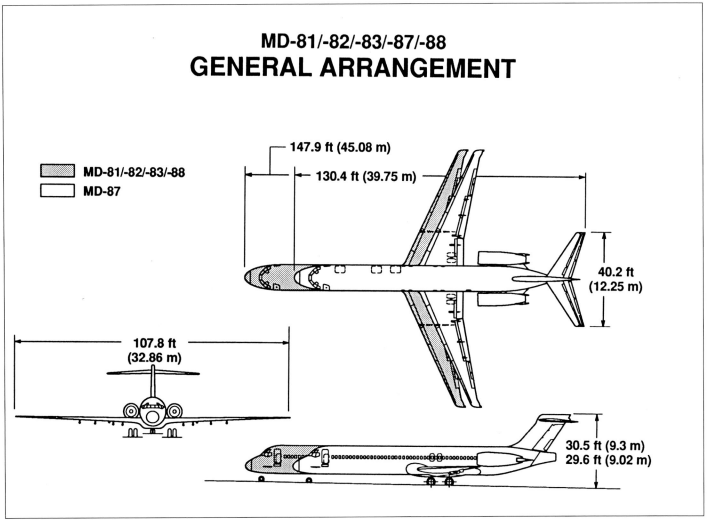

MD-81/-82/-83/-88
MD-87

147.9 ft (45.08 m)

130.4 ft (39.75 m)

40.2 ft (12.25 m)

107.8 ft (32.86 m)

30.5 ft (9.3 m)
29.6 ft (9.02 m)

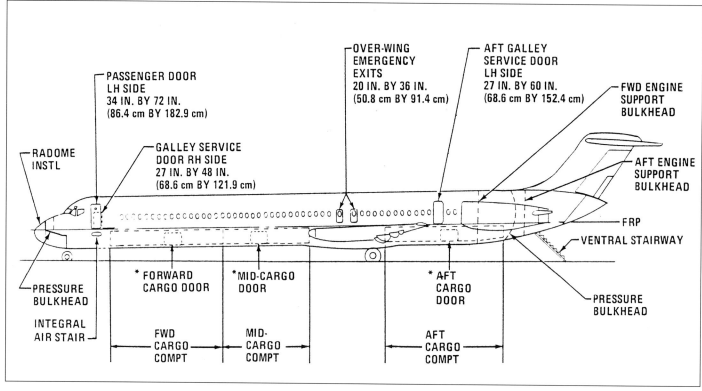

OVER-WING EMERGENCY EXITS 20 IN. BY 36 IN. (50.8 cm BY 91.4 cm)

AFT GALLEY SERVICE DOOR LH SIDE 27 IN. BY 60 IN. (68.6 cm BY 152.4 cm)

PASSENGER DOOR LH SIDE 34 IN. BY 72 IN. (86.4 cm BY 182.9 cm)

FWD ENGINE SUPPORT BULKHEAD

RADOME INSTL

GALLEY SERVICE DOOR RH SIDE 27 IN. BY 48 IN. (68.6 cm BY 121.9 cm)

AFT ENGINE SUPPORT BULKHEAD

FRP

VENTRAL STAIRWAY

PRESSURE BULKHEAD

* FORWARD CARGO DOOR

*MID-CARGO DOOR

* AFT CARGO DOOR

PRESSURE BULKHEAD

INTEGRAL AIR STAIR

FWD CARGO COMPT

MID-CARGO COMPT

AFT CARGO COMPT

While the internal requirement to maintain a common pilot type rating among the DC-9 series of aircraft has limited changes and improvements, the Long Beach designers did what they could to ease pilot workload and improve situational awareness. The addition of the IAE V2500 engines is another improvement.

TRAINING

Transition training from other airliner types was discussed with the Federal Aviation Administration (FAA), and it was felt that any pilot switching from the MD-88 to the MD-90 would only require less than one day of training. The FAA flight test pilots assigned to the MD-90 programme were proficient in six hours. Transition training from other MD-80 series airliners involved five days of ground school and a proficiency check with two landings. Pilots new to the DC-9 Series would take 102 hours of ground and simulator training.

PASSENGER OPINION

The McDonnell Douglas MD-80 twin-jet in comparison with the Boeing 727 and 737 won praise from airline passengers the world over. Results from five separate passenger surveys were remarkably similar, with the MD-80 consistently earning high marks for its personal roominess, ride quality, quietness, and cabin decor. More than 90 percent of 19,000 passengers surveyed in the United States, Europe, the Middle East and South America between 1981 and 1983 rated the MD-80 as 'appealing'.

Surveys conducted by independent researchers in the USA that were co-sponsored by McDonnell Douglas and airlines who operate MD-80s and competing airliners, showed MD-80 preferences of 3-to-1 over the Boeing 727 and nearly 8-to-1 over the Boeing 737. Under different passenger and service conditions in Europe and the Middle East, an Austrian Airlines survey found that air travellers reaffirmed preferences for MD-80s by wide margins.

McDonnell Douglas survey guidelines and objectives were to compare air travellers' experiences in MD-80 and Boeing 727 and 737 airlines, and to validate strong MD-80 preference by surveying a variety of airlines, locations, economy and first-class interiors, and passenger profiles. The method used involved interior feature ratings of the 737, 727 and MD-80 taken only from passengers flying in those aircraft. Preference ratings were permitted only when respondents recognised names and had opinions about each aircraft being compared. Respondents were given counterbalanced versions of the questionnaire so responses were not weighed in favour of the Boeing 727/737 or MD-80 airliner. Interviews were conducted by trained research personnel from completely independent research companies.

On each flight, an interviewer chose a different three-row seat area for conducting the survey. As a result, co-operation rates were over 90 percent, and representative samples were obtained. Although a majority rated all interiors as attractive, the sleek contour and interior features of the MD-80 were rated 'very attractive' far more often than the Boeing 727 and 737.

The following three statements were released by the airline research department.

'In coach, the MD-80 was a big overall winner . . . definitely superior, particularly with regard to seat comfort, underseat storage and quietness.'

'Centre-seat MD-80 passenger liked their airliner more than window-seat Boeing 727 passengers.'

' . . . A widening margin in favour of the MD-80 with increasing travel. More than three times as many frequent flyers rated the MD-80 very good (38 percent) than the Boeing 727 (12 percent).'

Airline surveys independent of McDonnell Douglas involved a South American international carrier. Surveys taken in four different regions totalling more than 8,000 respondents were performed from December 1982 through March 1983. Survey routes differed in flight lengths — less than one hour to over three hours, direct or multistop connections, and mix of business, tourist, and ethnic background of travellers. About 93 percent of all respondents surveyed rated the MD-80 as 'very good' or 'good' after having considered various specific interior features. Comparative ratings to MD-80 were sought only when the respondent had prior experience flying Boeing 727 and 737. The MD-80 was preferred over the Boeing 737 by 8-to-1 and over the Boeing 727 by 6-to-1 when choosing among these three airliners.

The purpose of a survey carried out by a major US airline was to compare the MD-80 to the Boeing 727. The survey was conducted in June 1983 in five domestic markets. Total sample size was about 6,400 (over 3,000 each) in the MD-80 and the Boeing 727. The airliners surveyed were flown on the same routes with the same fares and were operated by the same airline. Over 90 percent of all coach respondents surveyed in the MD-80 rated their airplane as 'good' or 'very good', with about twice as many giving the highest overall rating when in the MD-80 — 46 percent compared to 23 percent in the Boeing 727.

MD-90 — MEETING AIRLINE NEEDS FOR THE 21ST CENTURY

From 4 August 1997, MDC Long Beach became the Douglas Products Division of the huge Boeing Commercial Aircraft Group. Many employees were extremely happy that the name 'Douglas' had been retained in the new title. The acquisition by Boeing of the MDC empire for $15bn was not declared anti-competitive and could proceed without changes. Though it cleared the transaction with no changes, the Federal Trade

ABOVE LEFT: Side view of Balair MD-82 HB-INR which was completed on 4 January 1985 and delivered on 1 February showing the old tail and drag cone. *Chris Doggett*

CENTRE LEFT: Fuselage structural arrangements. *MDC*

LEFT: Austrian OE-LML taken in 1987. *Chris Doggett*

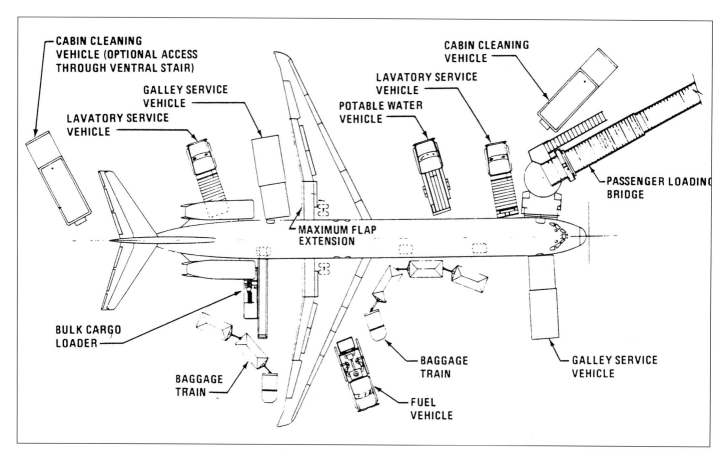

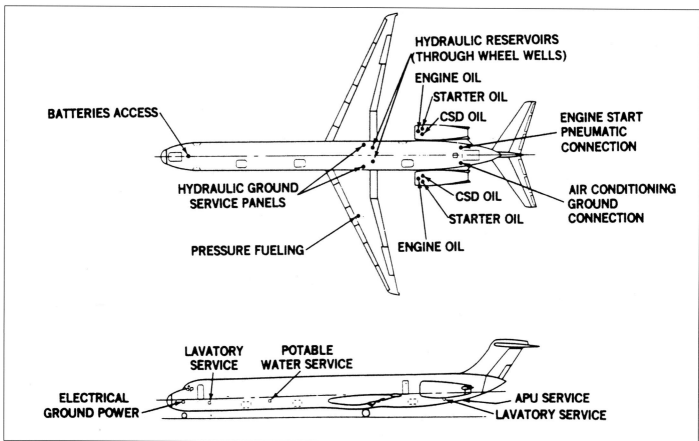

Top: Ground servicing equipment stations. *MDC*

Above: Ground service connections. *MDC*

Above Right: Cargo comparments and capacities. *MDC*

Centre Right: Seen at Zurich airport in May 1994 while leased to the now defunct Greek line Venus, MD-87 SX-BAV shows the forward baggage compartment doors open. *Mark Nutter*

Right: Cargo door and ground clearance diagram. *MDC*

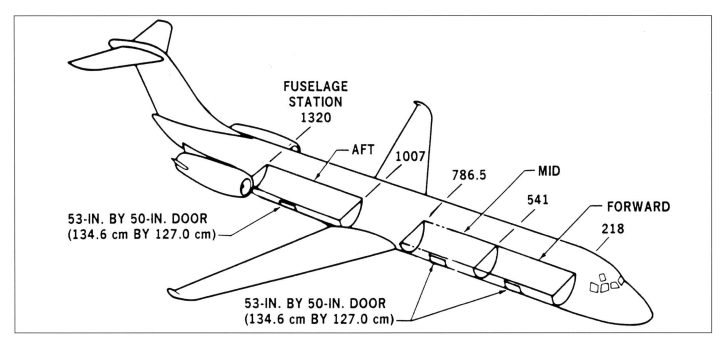

FUSELAGE
STATION
1320

AFT   1007   786.5   MID

541   FORWARD

218

53-IN. BY 50-IN. DOOR
(134.6 cm BY 127.0 cm)

53-IN. BY 50-IN. DOOR
(134.6 cm BY 127.0 cm)

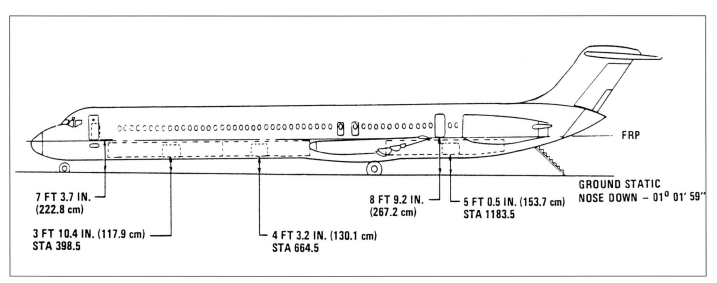

FRP

GROUND STATIC
NOSE DOWN – 01° 01′ 59″

7 FT 3.7 IN.
(222.8 cm)

8 FT 9.2 IN.
(267.2 cm)

5 FT 0.5 IN. (153.7 cm)
STA 1183.5

3 FT 10.4 IN. (117.9 cm)
STA 398.5

4 FT 3.2 IN. (130.1 cm)
STA 664.5

Commission (FTC) lent credence to the European Commission's concerns about the clauses that make Boeing the exclusive supplier to American, Delta and Continental Airlines for the next 20 years. It was evident that Boeing could become a

ABOVE: Any clutter of round dial instruments used in earlier MD-80 airliners has been lessened in the MD-90 by using an electronic flight instrument system (similar to that in the MD-88) plus a full flight management system and an electronic overhead annunciator panel. The wind shear computer and flight guidance and management systems have been modified for the MD-90. Because of the similarities between the various MD-90 cockpits air carriers are saving thousands of dollars in crew training costs. *MDC*

ABOVE LEFT: The MD-90 designation had applied to a number of series developments but when it came — first flying on 22 February 1993 — it was more than simply a stretched and re-engined MD-80. This is not to say the engines weren't unusual. They were IAE V2500 turbofans, replacing the Pratt & Whitney JT8Ds of the MD-80 family. Other major differences between the MD-80 and 90 were a new wing, a new APU, a lengthened forward fuselage and a new electrical generating system as well as a fully glass cockpit. Here SE-DMF shows off to good effect the new wing design on take-off. SAS took delivery of a batch of six MD-90-30 airliners. *IAE*

CENTRE LEFT: The main version is the MD-90-30, which is designated MD-90-30T when built in China. Here B-17915 is seen at Long Beach taking-off during acceptance flight trials. By the end of 1997 Uni Airways Corporation based in Kaoshiung, Taiwan, had taken delivery of six MD-90-30 airliners. *Michael Carter, Aero Pacific Images*

LEFT: The colourful *Orange County Flyer* (MD-90 N901RA s/n 53489 f/n 2129) belonging to Reno Air seen in landing configuration at San Jose, California on 1 December 1996. The airline operates 40 daily departures from its San Jose hub. The inaugural flight of the airline, Reno–Los Angeles took place on 1 July 1992 with an ex-Midway MD-82. By summer 1996 the fleet had grown to 29 airliners — eight MD-82s, 14 MD-83s, four MD-87s and three MD-90s. By March 1997 a further MD-87 had been added, bringing up the fleet to 30. *Edward J Davies*

$48bn aviation behemoth that controls almost 70 percent of the world's commercial aircraft market.

This event came just two years after Long Beach had celebrated the 75th anniversary of the founding of the Douglas Aircraft Company (DAC) and one of the events at the plant, to highlight the company's years of innovative commercial aircraft design, its latest twin-jet airliner, the MD-90, was delivered to Delta Air Lines during June. This was N901DA f/n 2100 s/n 53381 which first flew on 27 August 1993, being retained for test flying by MDC registered N902DC, and delivered to Delta at Atlanta on 5 June 1995.

Ronald W Allen, Chairman, President and Chief Executive Officer of Delta, said:

'The MD-90 is an aircraft designed for Delta's future. From the start, we participated in writing the specifications for this aircraft in anticipation of where our industry and our company are headed.'

Commencing in 1989 the airline had assembled teams of its employees to funnel information and design suggestions to MDC design teams at Long Beach. Witnessing the results of the combined five-year effort, Delta placed a firm order for 31 MD-90-30s with an option for an additional 106. By March 1997 19 MD-90s were registered to Delta, with a follow-on of 12 additional airliners taking deliveries into 1998.

The plan for the MD-90 was to re-engine the most advanced airliner in the successful MD-80 series, the MD-88, so that it would be capable of meeting anticipated Stage 4 noise reduction levels, reduce the interior cabin noise, increase fuel efficiency and cut down on the level of exhaust emissions. The teams sought to do this while maintaining the same pilot type rating as the MD-80 series and addressing the items that involved service delays.

When the two companies met, the airline presented Long Beach with a list of 10 problem areas affecting dispatch reliability. If these problems could be resolved then MDC would have one of the most reliable airliners in the world. With delays per 1,000 departures in parenthesis, the most recurring items included:

AC (Alternating Current) Generation and Control (0.45)
The auxiliary power unit (APU) (0.37)
Nose landing gear (0.30)
Digital Flight Guidance Computer (0.28)
Landing Gear Position Indicator (0.27)
Main landing gear wheels and tyres (0.26)
Stall warning system (0.25)
Compass system (0.25)
Main brake control (0.24)
Engine fuel control (0.24)

MDC design engineers quickly resolved the problems Delta had posed. First, the electrical system was replaced with a modular VSCF (Variable Speed Constant Frequency) system to prevent power surges and extend the service life of other electrical components. To meet the increased task of the aircraft's upgraded systems and new engine, MDC selected the Allied Signal/Garrett 131-9(D) auxiliary power unit. New software was introduced especially for the Digital Flight Guidance Computer and the stall warning system was upgraded. The compass system's problems were eliminated by the installation of an Inertial Reference System (IRS) and a new engine electronic controller solved the fuel control problem.

The remaining problems were associated with the landing gear. New 21in (53cm) wheels and tyres were added as well as a new spray deflector for the nose wheel. The brakes were replaced with carbon units reducing total aircraft weight by 400lb (181kg). Also incorporated was an independent dual brake valve system featuring digital anti-skid controls, a brake temperature monitoring system and in-flight ram air cooling. The landing gear position indicator had a new modified lens cap assembly installed.

COCKPIT

After accepting Delta's main problems, the team of MDC development engineer designers concentrated on refining the MD-90 cockpit to incorporate the latest technology. This was not a great challenge as MDC had specifically modified the MD-80 cockpit to a digital system for Delta when the airline ordered the new MD-88 in January 1986. One quote considered the new MD-90 as a 'third generation DC-9' being similar enough to the MD-88 that it offered Delta a tremendous saving in pilot transition and recurrency training costs as the flight deck layout is very similar.

The MD-90 retains the MD-88 Electronic Flight Instrument System. Improvements made to existing equipment include a better Flight Management System (FMS) and solid-state engine and systems displays, new software to drive the windshear computer, plus a solid-state overhead annunciator panel, and ARINC 700 Series avionics upgrade. Other new equipment in the cockpit includes an auxiliary control system, a Master Caution and Warning computer, an Air Data computer, and the Inertial Reference System (IRS). All these increase cockpit systems reliability and reduce maintenance while minimising possible errors and crew member workload.

Structurally the new MD-90 maintains the fuselage of the MD-83 with the addition of a 57in (145cm) plug forward of the wings, maintaining the Douglas tradition of stretching the fuselage of its airliners. The MD-90 incorporates a strengthened MD-83 wing while the tall tail unit and horizontal surfaces are from the MD-97. This installation also features a powered elevator and rudder capable of reverting to manual control. The ailerons remain unboosted and trim tab flown.

A new vacuum lavatory system has been installed in the MD-90. This offers single-point servicing so reducing aircraft turn-around time and possible airframe corrosion. In a weight-saving exercise, and to increase the reliability of some components, composites were used in 25 structural areas from the rudders, ailerons and trim tabs to the wing fillet fairings, tail cones and the floors and liners of the cargo compartment.

To allow Long Beach to use its huge shopfloor space more efficiently and to reduce manufacturing costs and streamline the twin-jet airliner assembly process, MDC introduced a modular assembly concept which includes the MD-90. Sub-assemblies of major fuselage sections can be accomplished off-site where the fuselage panels and other parts will be delivered from subcontractors. The components come together to form a module such as the nose section or forward fuselage. These modules are then transported to Long Beach for final assembly where they are attached as required to other sections to form a complete airliner shell. This also allows the plant to manufacture both the MD-80 and MD-90 series on the same assembly line.

IAE TURBOFAN

There is no doubt that the second key to the success of the MD-90 came with the wise selection of the International Aero Engine (IAE) V2525-D5 engine from the consortium of Pratt & Whitney (USA), Rolls-Royce (UK), Fiat Aviazione (Italy), MTU (Germany), and JAEC (Japan). The mating of this turbofan to the proposed MD-90 in the development and design stage confirmed MDC had a product that will still be in production well into the 21st century.

Grace M Robertson, vice president and general manager of the MD-90 twin-jet airliner programme confirmed that MDC was offering only the V2525-D5 engine for the MD-90. Robertson said that

'The decision to only offer one engine type was made with an absolutely firm conviction that this was the best engine and that there wasn't anything near it. We are willing to take the risk of being exclusive on this decision because there really wasn't a competitive engine as good. I believe that more every day.'

The V2500 series of turbofans is reputed to be 10 percent more efficient that the JT8D series which powers the MD-88. At current jet fuel prices, Delta forecasts that they will save $200,000 per year, per aircraft when compared to the fuel bill of an MD-88. This was confirmed by IAE President Robert Rosati who said,

'Experience has shown that the V2500 will save Delta money in operating costs, while providing the reliable, on-time performance passengers expect. It's a rugged, dependable engine that incorporates the best technology from around the world.'

ENVIRONMENT

With many European countries following the USA in regulating engine exhaust emissions, it is claimed that the V2500 series produces less than one fifth of the pollutants as established by international aviation regulations.

The solution to reducing the MD-80 series noise signature, begun with the new turbofan, is further reduced by the rear fuselage engine mounting — common to all DC-9/MD-80/MD-90/MD-95 series airliners. When integrated with an 'airport neighbour friendly' flight profile, the wing shields those on the ground from turbofan noise on final approach. The quiet airliner meets FAR 36 Stage 3 — ACAO Annex 16 Chapter 3 noise levels introduced for new aircraft designs. The Group Leader for Acoustics from the Aerodynamics and Acoustics Design and Technology group, Daryl N May PhD said:

ABOVE: One of the two prototypes of the MD-90 airliner seen in flight over the Sierra Nevada mountains in California during a routine test flight. The additional fuselage length accentuates the comparatively small wings of the MD-90. They are essentially the same wings as those on the earlier DC-9 airliner series. *MDC*

OVERLEAF, INSET RIGHT: By November 1990 more than 300 hours of wind tunnel testing had been completed on this model of the new MD-90, now in production at Long Beach. The model demonstrated aerodynamic characteristics of the new airliner powered by two International Aero Engine V2500 engines. It was installed in the 11ft (3.35m) transonic wind tunnel at the NASA Ames Research Center at Mountain View, California. The MD-90 first flew on 22 February 1993 and after FAA certification in late 1994, the first delivery to the launch customer, Delta, was made in February 1995. It entered revenue service two months later, and by March 1997 it was being used by 10 operators involving 46 aircraft. *Douglas*

OVERLEAF, INSET LEFT: The nose structure for the first production MD-95 airliner was laid down at Long Beach early in 1997. The MD-95 is similar in size to the successful DC-9 Series 30 and is being built in response to the growing 100-seat narrow body airliner market. It is powered by two BR715 turbofan engines which enable it to be quieter, cleaner and more efficient. The MD-95, redesignated Boeing 717, is designed for short-to-medium-range routes where larger aircraft are less economical to operate. *MDC*

OVERLEAF, MAIN PICTURE: In flight from Long Beach is MD-90-30 N901DC, the prototype that made the first flight. The new MD-90, now in service, is the quietest large jetliner and exceeds both US and IAE V25000 engines requirements. Production of the MD-90 is forecast to continue into the next century. *MDC*

'When we wanted to improve on the MD-80, clearly noise was one of the most important improvements we could bring to the design. The new engine brings improved economy and it may well bring improved reliability, but it also had to bring improved acoustical properties.'

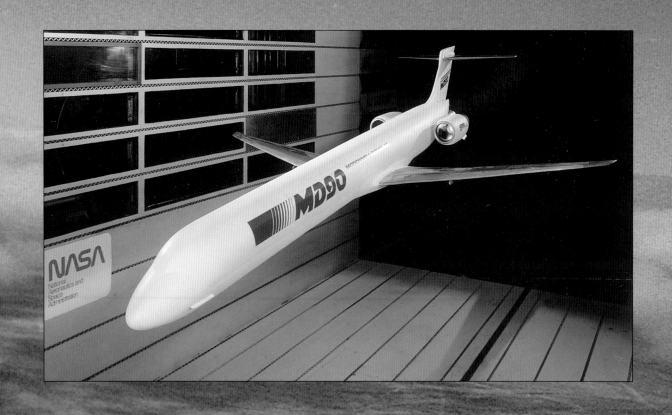

5 IN SERVICE

Within a decade of the MD-80's introduction, 64 airline operators across the world had taken delivery of airplanes of the series. Operators of both the Douglas DC-9 and the McDonnell Douglas MD-80 twin-jets are found mainly in Europe and the Americas, but also significantly in Asia. As well as these airlines — many of them long-time Douglas customers — can be added operators who briefly 'wet'-lease airliners. Among the many lease companies and operators are numbered some first-time buyers, with others acquiring pre-owned airplanes.

An increasing role is being made by the many leasing companies and banks which enables airlines to operate the very latest McDonnell Douglas product, without having to expend the vast sums of cash necessary today to purchase a new airliner. Quoted price for an MD-81 can range from $18m rising to near $30m, or even more for the very latest MD-88. The many leasing companies who have purchased quantities of the MD-80 series include Guinness Peat Aviation – Irish Aerospace, the Beverly Hills based ILFC, and Polaris Leasing of San Francisco.

Launch orders from Austrian Airlines (eight firm plus four options), Southern Airways (four firm and four options), and Swissair (15 firm plus five options) enabled MDC's announcement of a DC-9 Series 80 on 19 October 1977. It could have been known as DC-9-70 of Series 70, but with service scheduled for 1980, it was marketed as the Series 80 or Super 80.

Swissair and Austrian Airlines became the MD-80 series first operators. The first MD-81, HB-INC Thurgau f/n 938 s/n 48002, first flew at Long Beach on 12 August 1980 and was delivered on 12 September. Swissair's first MD-81 service was on 5 October 1980, from Zurich. It operated a total of 24 of the 114-seat, three-class MD-81s and in the spring of 1993 was scheduled to lease additional airliners from Guinness Peat Aviation, raising the MD-81 fleet to 26. By April 1997 Swissair had reduced its fleet to just nine MD-81 airliners.

The later MD-80 variants entered service as follows: MD-82 with Republic Airlines in August 1981, MD-83 with Finnair in July 1985, MD-87 with Austrian Airlines and Finnair in November 1987, and the MD-88 with Delta Air Lines in January 1988.

A joint launch customer for the MD-80 series was Austrian Airlines, which took delivery of its first MD-81 (OE-LDP

ABOVE RIGHT: Paramount Airways, a UK operator in the late 1980s, was the first British airline to operate the MD-80 using four 165-seat MD-83s. On take-off is G-PATD, today N9307R with TWA. *MAP*

RIGHT: The national airline of the Turkish Republic of Northern Cyprus is Kibris Turk Hava Yollari. Here is MD-90-30 TC-KTB delivered in March 1997. *Kibris Turk Hava Yollari/MAP*

Wien, f/n 924 s/n 4805) on 16 May 1981. The type commenced service between Vienna and Zurich on 28 October 1981, while the short-fuselage MD-87 variant opened a Vienna to Zagreb service on 17 December 1987.

It is interesting to note that OE-LDP was manufactured on 16 August 1979, then operated by MDC at Long Beach as N133727. It was re-registered N1002W in June 1980, a registration it carried on pre-delivery test flights before acceptance. By April 1997, Austrian was operating seven MD-81s, five MD-82s, two MD-83s and five MD-87s.

Pacific Southwest Airlines (PSA) was the first US carrier to fly the MD-80 — it began a service in California from San Diego on 17 December 1980, following a long association with Douglas products. A Douglas DC-3 opened PSA operations on 6 May 1949, operating between San Diego and Burbank, and the airline prospered with a DC-9 fleet. In August 1978 it ordered 10 MD-81s, the first of them delivered on 14 November 1980 (N924PS, f/n 946 s/n 48034, completed 15 July 1980 and named *City of Burbank* during 1988). The fleet grew to 20 MD-81s and 11 MD-82s, both in 150-passenger versions, but five more on order were cancelled.

California, Arizona, Nevada, New Mexico, Oregon and Washington were all served by the PSA MD-80s, through until 9 April 1988, when US Air took over PSA. The pathfinding MD-81 N924PS was re-registered N800US in October 1987 and is still in service with US Air.

The private Argentinian airline Austral Lineas Aereas, based at Buenos Aires-Aeroparque, has two MD-81s and two MD-83s. It took delivery of its first MD-81 (N10022, f/n 948 s/n 48024 named *Estrecho San Carlos*) on 8 January 1981. The airliner was completed at Long Beach on 15 August 1980. The 155-passenger MD-80s are scheduled mainly on the airline's busiest routes from Buenos Aires to Bahia Blanca, Cardoba, Mar del Plata, Mendoza, Rosario and Tucuman.

By the end of December 1997 the MD-80 inventory status revealed that no less than 1,150 of the series were in service with 61 operators worldwide. This consists of 96 MD-81s, 589 MD-82s, 1,232 MD-83s, 75 MD-87s and 158 MD-88s.

But pride of place for the largest fleet must go to American Airlines which has a fleet of 260 of the MDC airliners — 234 MD-82s, and 26 MD-83s. In October 1982, American picked up an offer from MDC to lease its initial MD-82s for two years. 67 MD-82s were bought by American in February 1984 and options taken on 100 more. With 165 MD-80s in service in 1989, American was calculated to have had the largest fleet of any single type of aircraft outside the former USSR, and it had 135 more MD-80s on order or option. Delta Air Lines is today second on the list with 120 MD-88 airliners in operation.

AIRLINER FINANCE

The list of DC-9 and MD-80 family operators is a lesson in geography, with airlines spread around the globe. To these can be added others who are 'wet' leased for short periods of time. Some have found a home with corporate owners, private companies and organisations, some first time buyers, others acquiring their airliners on the huge second-hand market.

Today there is an increasing role involving leasing companies and banks, all enabling airlines to operate the very latest expensive airliner, without having to expend the vast sums of money necessary for the purchase of new equipment. In the case of the MDC twin-jet airliners, the price can range from around $20million for the basic MD-81, to more than $30million for the sophisticated MD-88 with its updated avionics.

The list of companies world-wide involved in the leasing of commercial jet transports is voluminous and their airline business is difficult to record accurately month by month. In the 'A-Z' index of the world's major leasing companies, the first quoting the MD-80 series is Aeronautics Leasing Inc of Golden, Colorado, with one MD-82 acquired in November 1987 for lease to Northwest Airlines, whose 1996 airliner listing indicates nearly 50 airliners on lease from various companies large and small.

Possibly one of the largest leasing companies today is Ansett Worldwide Aviation Services based at Redfern, Australia and formed in September 1985 to manage the leasing of aircraft, plus purchase and resale of used aircraft. It has the MD-83 on its list with at least 10 on lease to TWA. GATX Air based in San Francisco has been operating since 1981, and by 1989 had MD-82s leased to both Alaska Airlines and TWA. Between 1981 and 1989 it handled a total of 23 MD-82 airliners.

MAJOR LEASING CUSTOMERS

The GPA Group, the Irish company built up from nothing over the past two decades by Tony Ryan, has today become one of the world's largest aircraft leasing consortiums. It manages a fleet of nearly 400 airliners covering a wide variety of modern types, including many from the MDC plant at Long Beach. The group makes more than half its profit selling aircraft, ranging from operating leases to third party investment.

Irish Aerospace Ltd, also based at GPA House, Shannon in County Clare, was formed in December 1984 by the GPA Group and MDC specifically to lease the MD-80 series airliner, each holding a 50 percent share. In November 1987 Mitsui of Tokyo acquired 25 percent of the MDC shares. By 1989 the company had 20 MD-83s in service with two MD-82s and 42 MD-83s on order from Long Beach, the latter deliveries extending to 1995. Airliners were leased to Korean Air Lines, Minerve and Spanair.

Blocks of MD-80 airliners are negotiated with MDC many months in advance of requirements for eventual lease to customers worldwide. Initially the Irish national registration EI is allocated to the new airliner and retained throughout a large number of leases involving a wide variety of airline liveries. Some are leased for short periods during the seasonal traffic periods.

The Polaris Aircraft Leasing Corporation of San Francisco is a subsidiary of the Polaris Holding Company of which 81 percent is owned by the General Electric Capital Corporation and 14 percent by the founder of Polaris, Peter Pfendler. Lease figures for 1989 showed eight MD-82/83/88 airliners in service with TWA, with 17 on order plus five options.

United Aviation Services (UAS) is a Panamanian registered company with international offices in New York, Paris and Geneva. It specialises in leasing, sales and financing of used Boeing and MDC airliners. The fleet summary for 1989 includes two MD-81s for Hawaiian Airlines.

Based in Beverley Hills, California, is International Lease Finance Corporation (ILFC), a company formed in 1973 by Leslie L Gonda its chairman, Steven F Udvar-Hazy its president and Louis L Gonda its executive vice-president. In 1983 the company made a public equity issue equivalent to 26 percent of the company's shares and ILFC concentration on operating leases. Leases which were current in 1989 included the MD-82 with one for Alaska Airlines, three for Continental, two for TWA, the MD-83 three for Air Liberté, one for Alaska, four for British Island Airways and one for British West Indian Airlines International (BWIA) the national carrier of the Caribbean islands state of Trinidad and Tobago.

AMERICAN AIRLINES

Established in 1934 and founded in direct succession to American Airways, formed in 1930, with other predecessor companies dating back to 1926, today American Airlines is one of the world's largest carriers, operating services to more than 164 cities throughout the world. Its current chairman and chief executive officer, Robert L Crandall, has been responsible for establishing marketing alliances with many other operators including China Airlines.

In the early 1980s American pinned its medium-term future to MDC by making the MD-80 series the object of what appeared the largest airliner order in history. It placed an order for 67 MD-82s, taking on option a further 100. It already operated 20 of the type under an operating lease agreement, taking delivery of a further 13 in 1984, so it was forecast eventually the fleet number could reach 200. This meant the airline would operate the largest airline fleet of any one type in the world, (with the likely exception of the former USSR). If all orders and options had been exercised, American's MD-80 fleet would have eventually reached a staggering 350 airliners.

In any case this was possibly representing the largest airliner purchase in history in terms both of the money involved and aircraft numbers. Unlike the first MD-80 deal American struck with MDC, the new order was an outright buy direct from the

ABOVE RIGHT: Japan Air System operates a varied fleet of airliners including the DC-9, DC-10, MD-80 and more recently 13 MD-90-30 airliners. Seen at Long Beach is JA 8004. *Michael Carter/Aero Pacific Images*

RIGHT: *Orange County Flyer* at Reno airport, Nevada, the home base for Reno Air which is now equipped with a number of MD-90-30 airliners. The airline also uses the MD-82 and MD-87. *Reno Air*

manufacturer. No financial details were released, although it is known that the MDC Finance Corporation was involved. United States airline analysts believed that the deal contained large price concessions for American.

It was estimated that the airline was paying between $18million and $20million per aircraft, whereas MD-80 sales at the time had been estimated at $24million to $26million an aircraft. It is known that when the first order for 20 twin-jet airliners was placed in September 1982 attached was a unique lease agreement with MDC whereby the manufacturer agreed to carry not only the cost of training, but also of major maintenance. In return for a low rental, American agreed to share the profits of its Boeing 727 and MD-80 fleet. The initial lease was for five years to enable the airline to transfer to an all-new 150-seat airliner. Consideration was rumoured at the time of American acquiring the new MD-90 or possibly re-engining its MD-80s.

The airline did not deny reports indicating that the terms of the agreement included attractive re-delivery payments, modest cancellation penalties, and improved terms on the existing leasing agreement covering the first 20 MD-80s. At a price of $20million in 1984, a firm order for 167 new aircraft would be worth some $3,300million.

There was a decision date for each group of MD-80s some 24 months prior to delivery. American was due to receive 25 aircraft in 1985 and 1986 and 17 in 1987 with an option open for eight more in 1987. From 1987 to 1991 the groups were reduced to 10 aircraft. This order took the MDC backlog of MD-80 deliveries to 150 aircraft.

The entire 176-aircraft order was to be worth some $764million to Pratt & Whitney: American would require a total of 382 JT8D-200 series turbofans including spares, and each engine was priced at $2million.

It was the intention of American to utilise its new MD-80 fleet, each fitted with 142 seats in a dual first and economy class layout, to expand its Dallas–Fort Worth and Chicago hub operations, and to increase its presence in transcontinental and strong business markets. Chairman Bob Crandall estimated the new MD-80s, together with new labour agreements, would cut operating costs to 19 percent. In 1984 American Airlines was operating into 108 airports in the United States with a mixed fleet of 244 aircraft. By January 1997 it was operating a fleet of 649 aircraft flown by a staff of 9,000 aircrew and in July 1997 retained 234 MD-82s and 26 MD-83s in that fleet. The first MD-82 N203AA completed on 14 January 1983, f/n 1097 s/n 49145, was delivered on May 12.

The impact of the American Airlines MD-80 order resulted in a further 1,000 staff increase at Long Beach during 1985, and increase in the production rate of more than 40staff. The 1984 employment figure at MDC Long Beach was quoted as approximately 12,000 with 6,500 working on the MD-80 programme alone. President Jim Worsham revealed that MD-80 production would increase from less than one airliner a week to 1.43 a week by January 1985.

The McDonnell Douglas Finance Corporation supports MDC at Long Beach in the marketing of the MD-80 airliner. It assists the manufacturer and its airline customers in structuring and negotiating the financing portion of aircraft sales. The MDFC has also aggressively sought business opportunities related to the MD-80 twin-jet airliner for its own portfolio.

During 1983, MDFC entered into lease transactions for five MD-80 aircraft which increased to 12 the number of MD-80s in its portfolio. Commercial aircraft leased during that year included MD-80s for New York Air, Pacific Southwest Airlines, and Midway Airlines. The finance company extended $93.5million of financing to airline customers in 1983, which represented the third largest aircraft volume year in the then 15-year history of the MDFC. As of 31 December 1983, the commercial aircraft portfolio included 55 owned MDC aircraft leased to airlines and aircraft-related receipts amounting to $106.5million.

MD-95 — WORLD'S BEST 100-SEATER

At least one Long Beach product now seems set to take the MDC tradition forward into the 21st century. The first Boeing 717-200, which started life as the MDC MD-95, was rolled out at the plant in June 1998.

In August 1994, MDC at Long Beach issued background information on the new MD-95 twin-jet airliner the company was offering to airlines. This 100-passenger airliner was designed to meet the need for an advanced technology aircraft built for short to medium range routes. It would be similar in size to the popular DC-9-30 series, of which 660 were built out of the total DC-9 production of 976.

First announced in 1991, the new design had a wing span of 93.3ft (28.7m) and an overall length of 119.3ft (36.4m). Maximum take-off weight would be 114,00lb (51.710kg) compared to 108,000lb (48.988kg) for the DC-9-30 model. Two versions were being offered: the MD-95-30 with non-stop range of 1,575 statute miles (2,535km) and the MD-95-30(ER) extended range with an optional auxiliary fuel tank for up to 2,024 miles (3,257km) non-stop service.

Like all the MDC twin-jet airliners, the MD-95 design has a five-across coach seating arrangement. It incorporates cabin features developed for the current larger MD-90 jetliner, including larger overhead baggage racks. The two-crew cockpit design features advanced technology systems developed for the MD-90, including an electronic flight instrument system, fully automatic flight management system and electronic displays for engine and system monitoring.

Power was to be provided by two BR-715 turbofan engines produced by the international consortium of BMW in Germany and Rolls-Royce in the United Kingdom. For the MD-95, the engine is rated at 18,500lb (82.2kN) of take-off thrust, with an increase to 20,000lb (88.96kN) possible for the MD-95-30(ER) airliner. The engine features lower fuel consumption, reduced exhaust emissions and significantly lower sound levels than the turbofans on similar-size airliners now in service.

Long Beach was thus offering to meet airline needs for fleet expansion in the 100-seat category airliner, and also as a replacement for hundreds of DC-9s still in service. It is interesting to note that as of July 1997 there were still 864 DC-9s in service with 70 operators. The MD-95 would also be able to replace other similar airliners being made obsolete by virtue of age plus stringent new regulations imposed on airport noise and engine fuel emissions. Deliveries were forecast to commence in 1998.

LAUNCH ORDER

In the autumn of 1995, an order for 50 airliners with an option for 50 more came from the US based ValuJet, which spurred the start of production on the MD-95-30. The over $1billion order came from this Atlanta-based low-cost carrier, formed in 1993 and offering low-fare scheduled jet services to short-haul destinations. A rumour that ValuJet had signed a letter of intent to purchase 25 Airbus A319 airliners in a $1.8billion deal was subsequently denied by Airbus Industrie.

Operations by ValuJet commenced on 26 October 1993 and the fleet by early 1996 included no less that 43 DC-9-32 airlin-

ABOVE RIGHT: On 18 June 1995 Saudia Arabia Airlines ordered no fewer than 29 MD-90-30 airliners from Long Beach. The largest air carrier in the Middle East Saudi operates international scheduled and charter services as well as domestic passenger and cargo operations. Shown at Long Beach towards the end of 1997 is HZ-APB performing taxi and braking tests during acceptance flight trials. *Michael Carter/Aero Pacific Images*

RIGHT: MD-83 D-ALLR was delivered to the Aero Lloyd on lease on 28 June 1991. Today the German carrier has 15 MD-83s.

BELOW: McDonald joined with the Swissair subsidiary Crossair and Swiss tour operator Hotelplan to provide the unique livery on MD-81 HB-IUH. Passengers flying aboard *McPlane*, as it was called, were even able to enjoy McDonald hamburgers on certain routes. *Crossair*

ers with a single-class seating for 113 passengers, five DC-9-21, four DC-9-31, one MD-81, two MD-82 and two MD-83s. There was a reduction in the fleet and no operations were flown between 17 June and 30 September 1996.

The airline anticipates the 100-seat MD-95-30 will provide a 7 percent cost per available seat mile advantage over the DC-9. On peak travel days the airline had been operating 236 daily system departures to 26 US destinations.

Announcing the launch order, John Wolf, executive vice-president of development at MDC Long Beach said:

'More than 500 people, including flight attendants, airline executives and a cross-section of passengers from around the world, evaluated the full-scale mock-ups of the MD-95 and we developed an evaluation process to identify cabin features considered most important. The new MD-95 interior features reflect that evaluators' response.'

Early in 1997 the nose structure was handed over for the first production MD-95, this being contracted to Korean Aerospace. A team of both national and international contract-partners from around the globe are supplying components and sub-assemblies to Long Beach, where the MD-95 is being constructed. Quality assurance and inspection, flight testing, and airworthiness certification will involve many many hours before the new airliner is turned over to any customer.

An announcement during August 1997 indicated that the airline title ValuJet had disappeared as the latter had purchased AirTran, a Boeing 737 operator, and was painting the twin-jet airliner fleet in AirTran livery.

THE FUTURE OF LONG BEACH

Long Beach, now having become a component of the huge Boeing Commercial Airplane Group, was due for change according to news released at the end of 1997. Boeing had decided to end production of the MD-80 and MD-90 in mid-1999, but would support the production of 50 MD-95s ordered by AirTran (ex-ValuJet). Seattle was to decide on the MD-95's long term 'regional jet' future, possibly including a 70-seat version in 1998, however it was already known that Boeing intended to cut the cost of producing this new airliner.

The removal of the MD-80 and MD-90 from the airline market — both of which it has been showing a gradual decrease in sales — was expected to benefit both the Boeing 737 and 757. The two Long Beach produced aircraft had a backlog of 104, mostly MD-90s. During 1997, only 16 MD-80s and 26 MD-90s were delivered.

A life-extension came, however, when an order for 24 MD-83s for TWA was announced on 21 April 1998, taking the estimated life of the Long Beach twin-jet assembly line to January 2000. The value of the TWA order is about $1.1billion (at list price). TWA had eight MD-83 deliveries pending from a previous order. But Boeing repeated its announcement that MD-80 and MD-90 twinjet production will be phased out when current commitments are met.

The new order will boost the TWA fleet to 103 MD-80s.

First delivery of the new MD-90-30 to the huge SAS fleet took place on 16 October 1996 with SE-DMF *Heidrik Viking*. Here LN-ROA *Sigurd Viking* one of SAS's eight MD-90-30s, is seen in landing sequence. *MAP*

TWA also operates 58 DC-9s. Each of its new MD-83s will feature 20 first-class seats in an overall 142 passenger capacity.

BOEING 717-200

In January 1998, Boeing announced that it had changed the designation of the Long Beach produced MD-95 to Boeing 717-200, bringing the twin-jet into the designation system of the Seattle-built commercial jet. Historians will recall with interest that the Boeing 717 designation was allocated to the military Boeing 707 known as the KC-135 Stratotanker. Ron Woodard, President of the Boeing Commercial Airplane Group was quoted as saying:

'The 717-200 is uniquely qualified to meet the evolving requirements of the new regional jetliner market. It's a 100-seat market that demands comfort, low operating costs and high schedule reliability. This is the plane to meet that need.'

The two-crew cockpit incorporates the industry's most modern and proven avionics technology configured around six interchangeable liquid crystal display units. The flight deck features include an Electronic Instrument System (EIS), a dual Flight Management System (FMS) and a Central Fault Display System (CFDS). In addition, Global Position System (GPS), Cat IIIb and Future Air Navigation Systems (FANS) are available as optional features. An advanced Honeywell VIA 2000 computer is also installed.

The MD-95/717-200 is designed to replace thousands of 100-seat aircraft now in service and to meet the needs for fleet expansion in the 100-seat category. The 129-passenger MD-95-50 with increased range capability is under evaluation as a follow-on model.

Way back in August 1996 it was revealed that an 80-passenger regional derivative was under study, and there have been indications that Boeing believe a 70 to 100 seat derivative of the MD-95 could be suited to the hotly contested regional commuter airliner market. Shrinking the Boeing 737 for this market would make it look like a 'fat cigar', according to one Boeing official, whereas the MD-95's narrower fuselage, with five-abreast seating and true stand-up headroom appears to offer a real advantage over competitors.

On 4 May 1998, Bavaria International Aircraft Leasing Company of Munich became the first European customer for the 717, when it ordered five 717-200s with deliveries scheduled in late 1999 and into 2000. The company said it saw considerable demand for 100-seaters, and there was no alternative model on the market — the 717, said Bavaria, was likely to find favour over turboprop aircraft still on the market. Later the same month, more than 30 European airlines and leasing companies attended a Boeing 717 awareness conference in Berlin, which Boeing saw as an encouraging indication of interest.

The first 717-200 was rolled out at Long Beach on 10 June 1998. Five airplanes were in final assembly at the Douglas Products Division and first flight of the 717 was expected in September 1998. Deliveries to customers were scheduled to begin in summer 1999.

6 AIRLINE OPERATORS

MD-80 CURRENT FLEET AND ORDERS

Operator	Code	81	82	83	87	88	Total
Aero Lloyd	XLL			11			1
Aerolineas Argentina	AR			1		6	7
Aeromexico	AM		11	7	3	10	31
Air Aruba	Z4Q			1		2	3
Air Jamaica	JM			2			2
Air Liberté	Zl1			8			8
Alaska Airlines Inc	AS		9	33			42
Alitalia	AZ		90				90
Allegro	ZXI			5			5
ALM-Antillean Airlines	LM		3				3
American Airlines Inc	AA		234	26			260
Ansett	ZT8			1			1
AOM-Minerve SA	Z9U			11			11
Austral	AU	2		2			4
Austrian Airlines	OS	5	5	2	5		17
Aviaco	AO					13	13
Avianca	AV			11			11
Avioimpex	M4A	1					1
Beiya Airlines	ZXZ		3				3
Blue Scandinavia	Z6K			1			1
C-S Aviation Services	CSV		3				3
China Eastern Airlines	VSA		13				13
China Northern Airlines	Z3N		16				16
Continental Airlines	CO	9	56	4			69
Crossair	LX	1	2	5			8
DAC	ZDC		2				2
Delta Air Lines	DL					120	120
Dinar	DIR	1		1			2
Edelweiss Air	Z11			3			3
Eurofly SPA	Z6R			4			4
Fairlines	FAN	2					2
Far Eastern Air	EF		7	2			9
Finnair	AY		10	12	3		25
Ford Motor Co Ltd	YFD				2		2
GE Capital Avn Services	GEC			4			4
Golden Nugget Aviation	ZGU				1		1
Great American Airways	ZGM				1		1
Iberia	IB				24		24
Japan Air System	JD	26			8		34
KEB Aircraft Sales Inc	Z49				1		1
Korean Air Lines	KE		11	3			14
Kuwait Airways	KUW			1			1
Meridiana	IG		9				9
Midwest Express	XYX					2	2
NKR (Delaware) Inc	NKR		1				1
North American Airlines	XGN			1			1
Northwest Airlines	NW		8				8
Nouvelair	Y6D			4			4
Onur Air	OHY					5	5
Otter Corporation	Z41			1			1
Reno Air	XQQ		8	14	5		27
SAS	SK	29	23	2	18		72
Spanair	Z9R		2	15	2		19
Sun Air	BVZ		3				3
Surinam Airways	PY				1		1
Swanair	Z50		7				7

Operator	Code	81	82	83	87	88	Total
Swissair	SR	1					1
Trinidad and Tobago	BW			5			5
TWA	TW		35	30			65
U-Land Grou	ZYU		6				6
US Airways	US	19	12				31
TOTAL AIRPLANES		**96**	**589**	**232**	**75**	**158**	**1150**

MD-90 INVENTORY STATUS

Operator	Code	30	30ER	Total
AMC Aviation	AMF		1	1
China Eastern Airlines	YSA	3		3
China Northern Airlines	Z3N	6		6
DAC	ZDC	3		3
Delta Air Lines Inc	DL	16		16
Eva Airways Corp	BRE	2		2
Great China Airlines	ZYK	1		1
Japan Air System	JD	13		13
Reno Air	XQQ	5		5
SAS	SK	8		8
KTHY	TC	3		3
Uni Awys Corporation	B7	6		6
TOTAL AIRPLANES		**66**	**1**	**67**

BELOW: Resplendent in the new colour scheme is TWA MD-83 N931TW at Miami, Florida, during 1996. Completed on 4 June 1987 it was delivered to Transpacific Enterprises Inc, being purchased by Ford Motor Credit Corporation, leased to Ansett Worldwide Aviation Service (AWAS) with a sub-lease to TWA, all on the same day — 10 July 1987. *Chris Doggett*

LEASING

ABOVE, RIGHT AND BELOW RIGHT:
There are scores of examples of
MD-80 series leases, sub-leases etc, far
too many to record in detail. Often this
also involves a complete change of
airline livery and registration. These
three examples depict MD-83 f/n 1583
s/n 49629 whose history is a prime
example.

Completed 28 March 1989 as
EC-269 (RIGHT) for Irish Aerospace it
was delivered on 15 May and passed
on to Oasis Airlines the same day
where it was re-registered EC-EOY on
23 June. Returned to Irish Aerospace
on 4 November 1990 it was leased to
Aerocancun as VR-BMI on the same
day. On 14 October 1992 it was
sub-leased to Private Jet Expeditions
in the USA and in December 1993 it
was sub-leased to Oasis again
becoming EC-525, then EC-FVB
(BELOW RIGHT) in March 1994.
Currently it is HB-IKP (ABOVE) with
Edelweiss, still under the original Irish
lease. *MAP*

ABOVE: This MD-82 PJ-SEH, f/n 1452 s/n 49661, photographed at Miami in 1993 was completed on 7 February 1988 as N11843 for Texas Air but not taken up. Sold instead to GPA Group Ltd as EI-BTY it was again not taken up. It then went to GPA as EI-BWB on 10 March 1988 and leased to ZAS Airline of Egypt becoming SU-DAK on 20 April. It was leased again to Spanair as EC-421 on 12 April 1990 and re-registered EC-EVY on 1 July. Back to GPA on 12 April 1991. It was then leased to ALM on 23 May. *Chris Doggett*

LEFT AND BELOW LEFT: Often the lease of an MD-80 airliner involves it being ferried from one far-flung continent to another. This is illustrated by these two examples taken from Europe (Austria and Switzerland) for service with Dinar Lineas Aereas in Argentina, a small domestic operator also flying regional flights to Chile, Uruguay, Paraguay etc.

MD-83 OE-LMD (LEFT) was delivered to Austrian Airlines on 28 March. It departed Vienna on 14 December 1996 for a winter lease, returning on 23 April 1997.

MD-82 HB-INW (BELOW LEFT) was delivered to Balair on 18 September and also leased to Dinar; note the more modern colour scheme. *MAP*

AEROLINEAS ARGENTINA

ABOVE: Based in Buenos Aires, Argentina, Aerolineas Argentinas is the country's flag carrier, operating extensive scheduled passenger and cargo services. Established in May 1949, it today operates a fleet of over 30 modern airliners including one MD-83 and seven MD-88s. Shown above is an earlier MD-82, LV-VBY, which was completed in July 1992 and delivered 11 December. The airline took delivery of three MD-82s originally destined for Austral, a local associate line, but not taken up, LV-VBX, LV-VBY and LV-VBZ. *MAP*

BELOW: The Argentine Government allowed privatisation of the national carrier in 1989 and Iberia acquired initially 30 percent, later increasing to over 80 percent. As well as a main base at Buenos Aires, Aerolineas has a hub across the Atlantic in Madrid, Spain. Shown is MD-82 LV-VBZ, completed in September 1992 and delivered on 11 December. *MAP*

BELOW RIGHT: LV-VGC f/n 2064 s/n 53447 belonging to Aerolineas Argentinas was completed in May 1993 and delivered to Argentina on 9 July along with LV-VGB f/n 2046 s/n 53446 which was completed in February 1993. *MAP*

AERO LLOYD

ABOVE RIGHT: Aero Lloyd, a Frankfurt-based airline, operates 15 MD-83s and has operated the MD-82 and MD-87. The first MD-83 with 167 seats entered service in May 1986, this being followed by 137-seat MD-87s during summer 1988. Seen here at Düsseldorf during 1996 in a new colour scheme is MD-83 D-AGWC. *Chris Doggett*

RIGHT: Aero Lloyd MD-83 D-DALE, completed 19 February 1987 and delivered to the airline on 28 March. It was first seen at Frankfurt during August 1997 carrying advertising for 'Trigema' the German sportswear company. Up to December 1996 this airliner had flown 29, 506 hours and completed 12,220 landings. During December alone it flew 233 hours with 97 landings. *Aero Lloyd*

AEROMEXICO

MAIN PICTURE: Seen at Miami in 1996 AMO MD-82 EI-BTX was completed January 1998 as N59842 for Texas Air Corp but not taken up. It instead went to Aeromexico on 9 October 1990. AMO (Aerovias de Mexico) is one of the country's two national airlines and is based at Mexico City. It is interesting to note that, although the earlier DC-9s carried 'XA' Mexican registrations, the MD-80s series carries either US or Irish registrations. By 1991 the combined DC-9/MD-80 fleet was approaching two and a half million landings in Aeromexico service. *Chris Doggett*

INSET: *Baja California Norte*, MD-82 N10033, seen at Miami during 1995. During December 1989, Aeromexico took delivery of the first two of 10 MD-88s, the most advanced of the MD-80 series. By July 1997 the airline was operating 11 MD-82s, six MD-83s, two MD-87s and 10 MD-88s. The Mexican carrier uses the MD-88s on domestic routes and on international service to the USA, in a spacious two-class configuration with 20 first-class passengers and 115 in economy. *Chris Doggett*

AIR ARUBA

TOP: Air Aruba, the national carrier of Aruba, was established in September 1988 by the Aruban Government initially as a ground handling agent. It is based at Beatrix International Airport, Reina Beatrix, Aruba, Dutch Caribbean and commenced operations on 18 August 1988. Its fleet includes one MD-83 — P4-MDE, ex-EI-CEH leased from GPA — and two MD-88s, N11FQ, ex-P4-MDA, and N12FQ, ex-P4-MDC, both leased from Polaris. This is N11FQ seen at Miami in 1994. *Chris Doggett*

AIR JAMAICA

ABOVE: Air Jamaica was established as the national flag-carrier late in 1968 commencing operations on 1 April 1969 with two new DC-9 airliners. A look at the MD-83 production list reveals that Ansett Worldwide Aviation Service, one of the world's largest aircraft leasing companies and based in Australia, reserved a block of MD-83s from s/n 53182 to 53192. Depicted is N870GA in new Air Jamaica livery. *MAP*

AIR LIBERTÉ

ABOVE: Air Liberté is a French carrier operating charter passenger services to both European and Mediterranean holiday resorts. By July 1997 the airline was flying eight MD-83s. It commenced operations in April 1988 with a single MD-83 leased from the GPA Group. Here is MD-83 F-GHHO which was completed on 24 February 1991 and delivered on 29 March. It is shown at Palma, Majorca during 1994. *Chris Doggett*

ALM ANTILLEAN AIRLINES

BELOW: In October 1982 ALM Antillean Airlines added two MD-82s to its DC-9 fleet, followed by a third leased from Continental in April 1988. Shown in an early colour scheme is PJ-SEF *Kibrahocha* which was completed on 27 May 1982 for Republic but not taken up. It was delivered to ALM on 4 October 1982. *Chris Doggett*

AIRTOURS

ABOVE LEFT: Striking study taken over the Sierra Nevada mountains near Long Beach shows MD-83 N30016 at the end of 1990. It was completed in November to become one of eight MD-83s operated by Airtours, a Manchester-based UK passenger charter carrier. Operations started in 1991 with five airliners leased from Irish Aerospace, N30016 being leased as G-TTPT on 15 March 1991 and named *Ben Crossland*. *Airtours*

BELOW LEFT: Excellent publicity photo taken at Manchester airport depicting the Airtours fleet of five MD-83s plus the operations personnel. The airliners are G-DCAC, G-HCRP, G-COES, G-TTPT and G-DEVR. A range of up to 2,500 miles (4,023km) was quoted carrying 167 passengers and seven crew. The carrier ceased operating the type in 1996. *Airtours*

ALASKA AIRLINES

ABOVE: Seattle-based Alaska Airlines became the first operator of the new extended range MD-83 when it signed for nine aircraft in March 1983. By July 1997 the airline had nine MD-82s and 33 MD-83s. The first commercial service was operated on 20 Febraury 1985 on the popular Anchorage–Seattle route. This is MD-83 N945AS seen landing at San Jose, California on 13 September 1996. *Ed Davies*

BELOW: Alaska Airlines took over Jet America, a Long Beach-based MD-82 operator, in November 1987. The current MD-80 Alaska fleet seats 135 passengers in a two-class configuration which includes first class. Shown is MD-83 N961AS which was delivered to Alaska on 31 March. It is shown at San Francisco on 27 June 1996. *Ed Davies*

AMERICAN AIRLINES

RIGHT: By July 1997 American Airlines was operating 234 MD-82s and 26 MD-83s on its extensive route system across the USA. The initial order was placed in September 1982 in a unique lease agreement with MDC. Today American Airlines operates the largest airline fleet of any single type in the world, outside the Commonwealth of Independent States (CIS). There was a time when, if all its commitments to the MD-80 series had been exercised, the fleet could have reached a staggering 350 twin-jet airliners. This is MD-83 N210AA completed in July 1992 and delivered on 20 August. By December 1996 this airliner had flown 41,847 hours and made 23,698 landings. *MAP*

ALITALIA

BELOW: MD-81 I-DAVK *Pompeii,* designated 'Super 80' on the engine nacelle, belongs to Italy's national airline Alitalia. The aircraft was completed on 8 May 1987 and delivered on 23 June. Alitalia has been a prolific DC-9 operator since it acquired the first of its DC-9-32s on 8 August 1967. Today the fleet includes no less than 90 MD-82s fitted out to carry 155 passengers in dual class, or 172 in single economy class. *MAP*

ALISARDA

BELOW RIGHT: Alisarda was formed on 24 March 1963, with the sole aim of developing tourist services to Coasta Smeralda in Sardinia. This leading Italian private airline was renamed Meridiana in September 1991. The fleet, which included six MD-82s, was transferred from Alisarda, the first having operated since 1984. The airline with its 175-seat aircraft operated a regular schedule as well as seasonal services to and from most cities in Italy, Switzerland, France and Germany, commencing in May 1966 after a period as an air-taxi and charter operator in Sardinia. The first two airliners were flown from Long Beach with Swiss registrations, these being HB-IKK on 20 September 1984 and HB-IKL on 27 September. These airliners are today registered I-SMEL and I-SMEM with Meridiana. Depicted is I-SMEP, delivered on 21 August 1989 and seen at Gatwick in 1990. *Chris Doggett*

AOM-MINERVE SA

ABOVE: The French government, in order to make room for Air France and Air Inter Europe at newly refurbished Orly Airport Ouest (West) terminal in Paris, decreed that AOM French Airlines must move to older and less competitive Orly Sud (South) terminal, used mainly by non-French carriers. AOM rebelled. Striking out they painted in French 'I want to stay at Orly West'. MD-83 F-GRMH is seen at Orly with its protest message. *MAP*

BELOW: MD-83 F-GGMD completed 23 June 1989 has a typically complicated history. It was delivered to Minerve on 21 July, leased to Jet Alsace the same day, returned to Minerve on 1 March 1992 and to AOM on merger the same day. By 1994 AOM French Airlines was operating five MD-83s with a further three more on order. *MAP*

AUSTRAL

ABOVE: Austral Lineas Aereas is a privately owned Argentinian airline operating a network of scheduled passenger services radiating from Buenos Aireas-Aeroparque. By July 1997 Austral was operating two MD-81s and two MD-82s both 155-passenger airliners. Here is MD-83 LV-WGN, which was completed in August 1990 and delivered as N907MD to Tish Aerospace prior to lease to Austral on 29 September. It was re-registered LV-WGN in September 1994. *MAP*

AUSTRIAN AIRLINES

BELOW: Austrian Airlines commenced services with the MD-81 on 16 October 1980, and with MD-87 on 17 December 1987. By May 1997 Austrian Airlines was operating a galaxy of the MD-80 series including five MD-81s, five MD-82s, and five MD-87s. Shown is OE-LMB *Eisenstadt* completed as an MD-81 on 16 Sepember 1985 and delivered on 20 October. In March 1991 it was converted to MD-82 configuration. In this photo MD-81 is stencilled on the engine nacelle. *Chris Doggett*

AVIACO

LEFT: Aviaco (Aviacion y Comercio) of Madrid, Spain, was formed in 1948 as a private company by Bilbao businessmen. Today the airline operates services throughout Spain and the Balearic and Canary Islands on behalf of Iberia. The 155-passenger MD-88 airliners, of which 13 are currently operated, were the first of this Long Beach model to operate in Europe.

During 1996 the airline unveiled a modified colour scheme by adding images of bicyclists over the cheat line. These were to celebrate the 1996 Vuelta — the annual Tour of Spain bicycle race. The bicycle colour scheme appeared on at least three Aviaco MD-88 airliners: EC-FOF, EC-FOZ and EC-FPJ *Rio de Vigo*. *MAP*

AVIANCA

BELOW LEFT: *Cuidad de Barranquilla* in the huge hangar at Shannon during an overhaul. EI-CBY was leased from GPA; after completion in June 1991 it was stored at Mojave, California, prior to lease to Avianca on 12 February 1992. During the last four months of 1996, Avianca had five MD-83 airliners processed through the Shannon Aerospace hangar for 15,000 flight hour checks. *Shannon Aerospace*

BALAIR

BELOW: Balair, Switzerland's largest charter airline, had at one time an all-Long Beach built fleet which included three MD-82s, one MD-83 and four MD-87s. All were fitted out for 149-passengers in a two-class configuration. Taking-off is MD-83 HB-IUL. *Chris Doggett*

BWIA INTERNATIONAL

BOTTOM: The national carrier of the Caribbean state of Trinidad and Tobago had a fleet of nine MD-83s by 1994. This one is MD-82 N9801F, which was leased to BWIA on 24 June 1985 for six months from Frontier Airlines and whose livery it carries with BWIA titles. *MAP*

BLUE SCANDINAVIA

BOTTOM LEFT: By December 1997 the Arlanda-based Blue Scandinavia was quoted by Long Beach as working only one MD-87 in its mixed fleet. Earlier it had operated four MD-83s and a single MD-87. Here is one of the MD-83s, SE-DHF. *MAP*

CANAFRICA

TOP: Canafrica Transportes Aereos was formed in 1985 with two 165-passenger MD-83s on lease from the GPS Group, and provided inclusive tour services in Europe. The airliners were maintained by Swissair at Zurich. In June 1988 the title Air Sur was adopted. Depicted is MD-83 EC-ECO completed 28 March 1987 and delivered via GPA to Canafrica on 28 April that year. *MAP*

CENTENNIAL AIRLINES

ABOVE: Centennial Airlines based in Palma, Majorca, operated up to six (all leased) MD-83s until November 1996 when the company ceased operations. Two were leased from Guiness Peat, two from Transwede and two from Tombo for

Finnair. EC-FIX first flew at Long Beach on 2 September 1986 and was registered SE-DHB for GPA for lease to Transwede. It went on sub-lease to Centennial as EC-389 on 29 March 1993, then was re-registered EC-FIX in June. *Rob Holder*

CHINA EASTERN AIRLINES

ABOVE RIGHT: Established on 25 June 1988, China Eastern Airlines based in Shanghai operates scheduled regional and domestic passenger services as well as cargo operations. Its large international fleet includes 13 Long Beach-built MD-82s and it has on order nine MD-90-30 airliners. Depicted on final approach to Hong Kong Airport during November 1996 is B-2102 completed 29 November 1982 and delivered to the airline on 1 May 1988. *Mark Nutter*

CHINA NORTHERN AIRLINES

BELOW LEFT: China Northern Airlines, based at Dongta Airport, Liaoning, was established in 1990 and today is one of six major airlines operating in China on scheduled, charter, regional and domestic passenger services over a network of 120 routes to Japan, Korea and South-East Asia. Its fleet of MD-80 and MD-90 airliners includes 18 SAIC China-built MD-82s. On approach to Hong Kong during November 1996 is B-2145, completed by Shanghai Aviation Industrial Corporation in August 1992 and purchased by China Northern Airlines on 20 October 1994. *Mark Nutter*

CONTINENTAL AIRLINES

BELOW: Continental is one of the largest US carriers, with an extensive network of scheduled passenger services covering over 80 domestic and nearly 50 international destinations. In June 1983 the airline placed its first order for a single MD-83, the records revealing that this was N72822 f/n 1309 s/n 49482, delivered originally for Texas Air Corporation but going to Continental on 30 September 1986. It is still in service today. N477AC, an MD-82, is seen at Miami during March 1987. Ex-Air California, N477AC transferred to Continental on 12 November 1986 on lease and is still in service over 10 years later *Chris Doggett*

CROSSAIR

ABOVE LEFT: Established in 1975, the Swiss regional and domestic airline Crossair has its base at Mulhouse-Basle with a hub at Lugano. Among its varied fleet are one MD-82 and seven MD-83 airliners. This MD-81, HB-INV, was leased from Orient. It was completed on 15 February 1987 and delivered to Swissair and named *Dubendorf* on 18 March. *Crossair*

ABOVE: Daily hangar scene at Shannon Aerospace who now utilise a new combi-dock which is custom-made to cater for almost any airliner including Boeing 737s, 757s, DC-9s, MD-80s and A320s. Seen in the huge hangar undergoing maintenance checks are Boeing 757 D-ABNX of Condor, Boeing 757 9A-CTC of Croatia Airlines, a Crossair MD-80 and a Sun Air DC-9 from South Africa. The airport at Shannon has become a major aviation centre and in the process the largest industrial site in Ireland. *Shannon Aerospace*

BELOW LEFT: McDonald joined with the Swissair subsidiary Crossair and Swiss tour operator Hotelplan to provide the unique livery on MD-81 HB-IUH. Crossair commenced operating the airliner exclusively for Hotelplan on 29 March 1996, on charters from Zurich and Geneva to Mediterranean resorts. Passengers flying aboard *McPlane,* as it was called, were even able to enjoy McDonald hamburgers on certain routes. *Crossair*

DELTA AIR LINES

RIGHT: Originally built as an MD-82, N905DL was completed on 29 January 1987 and delivered to Delta on 1 April. On 25 June it was bought by the Chrysler Capital Corp and leased to Delta on the same day. During August 1988 it was one of a number of the MD-82 Delta fleet returned to Long Beach for modification to MD-88 configuration. Today this Atlanta, Georgia, based airline has a fleet of 120 of the model. *MDC*

EDELWEISS

BELOW: During 1996, Edelweiss, a new Zurich-based joint venture between Venus Air and Kuoni, Switzerland, launched holiday charter flights to the Balearics, Canary Islands, Cyprus, Tunisia and Portugal. Named *Avosa*, MD-83 HB-IKN is seen at Zurich, formerly G-GMJM of Guiness Peat, who leased it to Air Tours in March 1992. *Chris Doggett*

FINNAIR

FAR RIGHT: Finnair, the national airline of Finland, by July 1997 was still operating 10 MD-82s, 10 MD-83s and three MD-87s covering an extensive network of scheduled services from Helsinki. It was the launch customer for the MD-83 and MD-87 when it replaced orders in February and December 1984 respectively. Depicted is OH-LMB, the second MD-87, completed on 1 December 1987 and delivered 8 January 1988. *Chris Doggett*

GERMAN WINGS

ABOVE: German Wings was an ambitious
Munich-based scheduled airline which
unfortunately ceased operations after just
one year. Four new MD-83s started
services on 10 April 1989, and four more
were added later in 1989 and 1990 on lease
from GPA and ILFC. This is MD-82
EI-BTX completed January 1988 as
N59842 for Texas Air Corp but not taken
up. It was sub-leased to German Wings on
1 March 1989. *MAP*

HELIOPOLIS

ABOVE RIGHT: Heliopolis, an Egyptian
based airline, operates a single MD-83
taken from a batch of 11 reserved by
Ansett Worldwide Aviation Services of
Australia. It is seen here in Helipolis's
smart livery . *MAP*

IBERIA

RIGHT: Iberia — Lineas Aereas de
España, the national airline of Spain —
by July 1997 was operating a fleet of 24
MD-87 airliners — a shorter member of
the ubiquitous MD-80 family, seating a
maximum of 109 passengers. MD-87
EC-EUC *Ciudad de Toledo* was completed
on 3 February 1990 as EC-292 and delivered on 30 March. It was re-registered on
10 July 1990. *Chris Doggett*

JET ALSACE

ABOVE: Founded in 1988, Jet Alsace based at Basle-Mulhouse Airport, started operating a Minerve MD-83 in July 1989. The airline was an affiliate of Minerve undertaking charters between Basle–Paris and to destinations on the Mediterranean. MD-83 F-GGMD was completed March 1988 and leased to Jet Alsace on 21 July 1989, being returned to Minerve on 1 March 1992. This was the day the airliner was transferred to AOM French Airlines with whom it operates today along with 10 other MD-83s. *MAP*

LINEA AEROPOSTAL VENEZOLANA

ABOVE LEFT: LAV — the government controlled airline — has operated variants of the DC-9 and acquired three MD-83s in 1986, these supplementing the dozen earlier DC-9s. Later the MD-83 fleet was increased to six. Here is MD-83 YV-39C, completed January 1988 and delivered on 26 February. In September 1994 it was withdrawn from use and stored at Caracas with 16,158 hours 15,756 landings on the airframe. *MAP*

JAPAN AIR SYSTEM

LEFT: MD-81 JA8296 was completed June 1990 and delivered 20 July. JA8297 followed on 20 August. JAS has operated the DC-9, MD-80 and the MD-90 series. The first order for five MD-81s was placed in August 1978, taking delivery from 30 January 1981 onwards. By July 1997 the airline was operating 26 MD-81s, eight MD-87s and eight MD-90s. *MAP*

LINEAS AEREAS CANARIAS

ABOVE: Shown in landing configuration is an unidentified MD-83 of the now defunct LAC — Lineas Aereas Canarias. This Tenerife-based airline had its first of five MD-83s —EC-EFU *Isla de Lanzarote* — delivered on 19 October 1987. This was followed by four more, all five being on lease from GPA. The airliners were used on passenger and cargo charters to the Canaries from points in Europe and North Africa, as well as on inter-island services. By 1992 the fleet of MD-83s had been returned to the GPA Group. *Chris Doggett*

MIDWAY AIRLINES

ABOVE RIGHT: Chicago-based Midway Airlines commenced flying operations on 1 November 1979 with three ex-TWA DC-9s. Rapid expansion followed as the network extended to serve more than 60 destinations in the USA and Canada plus the US Virgin Islands and the Bahamas. At one time it had a fleet of 120-seat MD-87s, two MD-88s, three MD-83s and four MD-82s, the last three types seating 143 passengers. All aircraft had eight first class seats. Shown here is MD-87 N8808ML. *Chris Doggett*

KOREAN AIR LINES

RIGHT: HL-7282 belonging to Korean Air Lines was completed on 30 June 1987 and delivered to Korea on 18 August; it is seen here in February 1995. Korean Air Lines was established on 1 March 1969 on scheduled passenger and cargo services. Its large fleet of airliners includes 11 MD-82s and three MD-83s. HL-7282 is seen at Seoul Airport, South Korea. *Mark Nutter*

NEW YORK AIR

ABOVE: New York Air operated a fleet of crimson MD-82s introduced in September 1982 on low-fare scheduled services out of New York's La Guardia and Newark airports. In February 1987 the airline was integrated into Continental and the airliners appropriately marked. Shown here is MD-82 N814NY, which was completed on 2 April 1982 as N480AC for Air California; it went to New York Air in August 1985. *MAP*

NORTHWEST AIRLINES

TOP: Northwest Airlines acquired a large fleet of Long Beach twin-jet airliners from its merger with Republic on 12 August 1986, making Northwest one of the world's largest airlines. By July 1997 it was still operating eight 143-seat MD-82s configured in two-class layout. Depicted at Miami in 1993 is MD-82 N314RC, which had been completed on 1 March 1982 as N1004L for Republic. *Chris Doggett*

NOUVELAIR

TOP RIGHT: Nouvelair, a Tunisian operator associated with Air Liberté, worked four MD-83s in July 1997, including EI-CGI (ex-EC-EKM) and F-GHEC (ex-G-PATC) both leased from Air Liberté. Here is the former, EI-CGI, which completed on 8 July 1988 as EC-178 for Irish Aerospace. Uniquely, the national registration letters 'TS' for Tunisia have never been used on the MD-80 fleet. *Chris Doggett*

OASIS INTERNATIONAL AIRLINES

CENTRE RIGHT: Oasis is a Spanish charter carrier based in Madrid operating in Europe during the summer holiday months, then during the rest of the year the airliners are operated by Mexico-based Aerocuncun. Oasis operated the MD-83 starting with a Malaga–Manchester–Malaga round trip on 27 May 1988. By July 1996 the airline was operating a single MD-82 and two MD-83s, the latter configured for 165 passengers, flying an extensive charter network from Madrid and Malaga. Depicted is MD-83 EC-EOM, completed on 14 March 1989 and delivered as EC-260 to Irish Aerospace. *Chris Doggett*

PACIFIC SOUTHWEST AIRLINES

RIGHT: PSA, a major US regional airline, took delivery of its first MD-81 on 18 November 1980. The fleet grew rapidly until it eventually numbered 20 MD-81s and 11 MD-82s (both configured for 150 passengers). On 9 April 1988 the airline was absorbed by US Air. Here is N825US, which completed on 30 May 1984 and was delivered on 30 June. It was named *The Smile of San Jose* and registered N949PS. *MAP*

ONUR AIR

LEFT: Onur Air (Anur Air/Hava Tasimacilik AS) became established and operational during 1992, is located in Istanbul with its main operating base at Antalya. The current fleet includes a variety of Airbus products plus five MD-88 airliners. This is TC-ONO, the remainder being TC-ONM, TC-ONN, TC-ONP and TC-ONR. The last were due for delivery in 1998. Photographed during take-off sequence at Long Beach during a test flight is MD-88 TC-ONN. *Michael Carter/Aero Pacific Images*

PARAMOUNT AIRWAYS

BELOW LEFT: Based at Bristol in the UK, Paramount operated a total of four MD-83s on lease from the GPA Group between April 1987 and August 1989. Unfortunately the airline encountered difficulties and a rescue package failed. It was the first British operator to use the MD-80 and the 165-seat aircraft were employed on inclusive tour flights. This is G-PATB, completed on 26 February 1987 as G-DAIO for the GPA Group but not taken up, becoming G-PATB leased to Paramount on 29 April 1987. *Chris Doggett*

PRIVATE JET EXPEDITIONS INC

BELOW: Based in Wichita, Kansas, Private Jet is not operating the MD-80 today but in the past has utilised a fleet of MD-83s on lease from GPA most of which retained their Irish registrations, plus one MD-83 (F-GHHP) from Air Liberté. Their other planes were US registered. One MD-87, f/n 1634 s/n 49777 N497PJ, was leased in December 1992 and one MD-82, f/n 1634 s/n 49144 N500TR, in March 1993. Depicted is N902PJ f/n 1357 s/n 49401 seen on take-off from Palma, Majorca in 1994. *Chris Doggett*

RENO AIR

FAR LEFT: Reno Air is a publicly owned US regional passenger carrier formed in 1992. In the past it has operated the MD-82 and MD-83, and now it operates the MD-90. Depicted is MD-82 N84ORA, which first flew on 12 June 1986 as SE-DFX *Ring Viking* for SAS. It remained in Scandinavia until February 1993. *MAP*

SCANDINAVIAN AIRLINES SYSTEM

LEFT: During 1996 SAS celebrated its 50th Anniversary resulting in this MD-87, SE-DIP *Margret Viking*, being appropriately decorated. It first flew on 3 October 1991 and was initially registered to MDC as N6202D. Allocated OY-KHS with SAS it was not originally taken up and eventually delivered as SE-DIP on 21 October 1991. It was bought by Obit Leasing International Company Limited on 8 November 1991 and leased to SAS the same day. *SAS*

CENTRE LEFT: SAS is the designated national carrier for Denmark, Norway and Sweden. It has been a prolific operator of the Long Beach-built twin-jets since May 1968 when it introduced the earlier DC-9 to its customers. The fleet registrations are divided between 'OY' Denmark, 'LN' Norway and 'SE' Sweden. Seen at Heathrow, *Aud Viking*, MD-81 LN-RML was completed 23 February 1991 and delivered on 15 March. *AP Photo Library*

BELOW: Currently SAS operates a fleet of 29 MD-81s, 23 MD-82s, two MD-83s and 18 MD-87s. It also operates the MD-90 airliner. Depicted in special publicity occasion livery is MD-82 LN-RLE *Kettil Viking*, which completed on 18 October 1985 and delivered eight days later. *MAP*

SPANAIR

ABOVE: By March 1997 Spanair was operating a fleet of 18 MD-80 series aircraft consisting of one MD-82, 15 MD-83s and two MD-87s. At least nine were leased, seven from GPA, one from AOM and one from Polaris. All were configured in an all-tourist layout for 163 passengers and heavily employed on the airliners charter programme which served all popular destinations in Spain and the rest of Europe. Inaugural flight took place on 1 June 1988 from Palma de Mallorca, its home operating base, to Bilbao. MD-83 EC-FXA is seen preparing for departure from Palma de Mallorca in 1992. *Chris Doggett*

SWISSAIR

BELOW: Joint cooperation between MD-80 operators is well known but not often advertised on the airliner itself. Shown is Swissair MD-81 HB-IND seen landing at Zurich in 1995. In addition to the words 'servus Wien' it also has 'Joint flight by AUSTRIAN SWISSAIR' inscribed on the lower part of the forward fuselage. HB-IND first flew on 6 October 1980 and was delivered to Swissair and named *Zug* on 26 October. *Chris Doggett*

SUN JET INTERNATIONAL

ABOVE: Based at St Petersburg, Florida, since it was established in 1993 by its parent organisation, Sun Jet Holidays Corporation, today Sun Jet operates a mixed fleet of Long Beach-built airliners — two MD-81s (both ex-Hawaiian) and a single MD-83 — ex-D-ALLD. Photographed at Orlando, Florida on 25 April 1997 is MD-81 N818SJ, which has been leased since 15 July 1993. It is ex-Hawaiian N839HA *Beautiful Hilo* which was delivered on 20 July 1981 after completion at Long Beach on 21 April. *George W Pennick*

SUNWAY

BELOW: TC-INC *Ersel*, seen at Dusseldorf, Germany during 1995, is a multi-registered Sunways Intersun Havacilik MD-83. It is one of four of Sunway's MD-83 airliners, all on lease from GPA. On leaving the factory in October 1989 it was registered EI-CKM, then successively D-ALLW, XA-RPH, EC-FFF, EC-733 and now currently TC-INC. *Chris Doggett*

TRANSWEDE

ABOVE LEFT: Transwede MD-83 SE-DPU, seen here at Gatwick in 1993, has had a chequered career. Completed on 20 October 1990, it was delivered as XA-RTK to Irish Aerospace on 18 December 1990. Many leases followed including one to Compass Airlines as VH-LNH on 3 August 1992. After re-possession it went on lease to Transwede on 25 May 1993 and then to Spanair as EC-592 on 12 March 1994, it was re-registered EC-FXA in June 1994. *Chris Doggett*

CENTRE LEFT: Formed early in 1985, Transwede placed an order for two MD-87s in July 1987. The first was SE-DHG, which was delivered on 4 August 1988. It was completed on 12 January 1987 and initially registered N287MD to Long Beach. It was leased by Transwede to Norway Airlines and then to Venus in 1993/94 becoming SX-BAW; it returned to Sweden on 2 January 1995. *Chris Doggett*

TUR EUROPEAN AIRWAYS

BELOW LEFT: Known locally as Avrupa Hava Yollari, TUR was a Turkish charter carrier based at Istanbul, operating inclusive-tour flights to destinations in Europe. When it started operations in April 1988 its fleet included two MD-83 airliners on lease from Irish Aerospace Limited. Both were returned after lease by January 1994 when the company ceased operations. The two MD-83s were TC-TRU (shown here) delivered on 30 May 1991, and TC-RTU delivered on 18 April 1992. *Chris Doggett*

TRANS WORLD AIRLINES

ABOVE: By March 1997 TWA was listed as operating 24 MD-83 and 30 MD-82 airliners plus a mixed fleet of 58 earlier DC-9 models. Its first in the MD-80 series, MD-82 N901TW was delivered on 18 April 1983. The 142 passenger airliner seats 12 first class and 130 economy class passengers and operates a huge domestic network serving both the Atlantic and Pacific seaboards on a hub and spoke system out of St Louis, Missouri, which is also the airlines' corporate headquarters. *TWA*

BELOW: On 30 November 1974 TWA officially launched a new colour scheme which replaced the earlier traditional 'twin-globe' scheme. Then, during 1996 TWA introduced a more futuristic colour scheme on its large airline fleet: shown in the new colours is MD-83 N9420D in position for departure from Runway 01R at San Francisco on 22 February 1997. *Edward J Davies*

UNIFLY EXPRESS

INSET LEFT: Founded in 1980 as a privately owned carrier, with its fleet consisting of two MD-82s and two MD-83s all leased from GPA, Unifly Express started operations with the type in 1988 on an *ad hoc* basis and contract passenger and freight operations out of Ciampino, Rome, to holiday resorts in Europe and the Mediterranean, even operating as far as the Canary Islands. The four MD-80 series airliners were MD-82s EI-BTX, EI-BTY, and MD-83s EI-BTU and EI-BTV. By March 1990 the four airliners had been returned to the GPA Group, and despite the purchase of the Italian regional airline Alinard Spa, no further airliners were leased. Illustrated is MD-83 EI-BTU. *Chris Doggett*

VENUS AIRLINES

ABOVE: Based in Athens, Venus was established during 1993. It operates one MD-83 but in 1994 had two MD-87s and two MD-82s. One of these went by June 1996, the other by February 1997. The two MD-82s were SX-BBV and SX-BBW, the former shown on approach to Athens airport in 1994. *Chris Doggett*

US AIR

INSET RIGHT: *The Smile of San Diego* is seen here in US Air livery at Fort Lauderdale, Florida during 1995. Registered MD-81 N818US it was completed on 17 February 1982 as N943PS for PSW. It was re-registered in October 1987 prior to the airline merger on 9 April 1988. *Chris Doggett*

US AIR

LEFT: Today one of the world's largest airlines serving almost 200 points in 36 US states, US Air's many acquisitions included Pacific Southwest in April 1988 when it took over 19 MD-81s and 12 MD-82s. Shown in early livery is MD-81 N817US, ex-PSW N942PS re-registered in September 1987. *Chris Doggett*

ZAKANI AVIATION SERVICE

FAR LEFT: ZAS is known as the Airline of Egypt and was formed in June 1982 obtaining a commercial passenger carrying license in September 1987. In March 1988 a single MD-82 was acquired — SU-DAK, on lease. This was followed by a single MD-82, two MD-83s and three MD-87s all fitted out for 167 passengers carried in a single-class layout. A scheduled Cairo–Amsterdam route was added to domestic service. ZAS ceased operations on 21 October 1995. *A P Publications*

BELOW: ZAS MD-82 YU-ANG, completed 14 May 1985 and leased from Inex Adria Airways from 5 January 1989 to 1 May 1989. *MAP*

7 ACCIDENTS & INCIDENTS

May 1980: MD-81 N980DC   Edwards AFB, CA, USA

Completed at Long Beach on 18 October 1979 this was the prototype MD-80 which first flew on that date. Trials proceeded smoothly with only the odd problem. However, during May 1980 N980DC was damaged in a heavy landing at Edwards Air Force Base, California whilst taking part in a new Federal Aviation Administration (FAA) test requirement to ascertain the minimum distance required from a height of 50ft (15m) to touchdown. There were no casualties among the flight test crew and the aircraft was repairable. However, N980DC was withdrawn from further use and placed in long-term storage at Grayson County Airport, Sherman, Texas. It was powered by two JT8D-217 turbofan engines and up to retirement had flown 3,065 hours and accomplished 6,558 landings.

19 June 1980: MD-81 N1002G   Yuma, AZ, USA

Completed at Long Beach on 26 June 1979 this was the second Series 80 airliner and made its first flight on 6 December 1979. Initially allocated the registration HB-INB with Swissair, it was not taken up and was finally registered N1002G and operated by the company. On 19 June 1980 it was damaged in a landing accident at Yuma, Arizona, during simulated hydraulic failure trials. It was repairable but the boom of a crane being used to move the airliner from the runway broke off and fell across the fuselage, causing additional damage and rendering repair uneconomic. It was powered by two JT8D-209 turbofan engines and had completed 373 flying hours and accomplished 364 landings.

1 December 1981: MD-82 YU-ANA   Corsica

Completed at Long Beach on 15 May 1981, this MD-82 was delivered on 11 August to the airline. On 1 December 1981 it crashed into Mont St Pietro, 25 miles (40km) south-east of Ajaccio, Corsica. There were 180 fatalities and no survivors. The airliner to that date had completed 663 flying hours and accomplished 470 landings. YU-ANA was powered by two JT8D-217 turbofan engines.

16 August 1987: MD-82 N312RC   Detroit, IL, USA

Completed at Long Beach on 15 October 1981, it became N1004F for Republic Airlines on 8 December 1982. Following a merger with Northwest Airlines on 1 October 1986 the fleet number became 9308. On 16 August 1987 it crashed on take-off from Detroit Airport with 154 fatalities and only three survivors. Powered by JT8D-217 engines the airliner had completed 14,928 flying hours and accomplished 8,975 landings.

Operating as Flight 255, the twin-jet airliner took off from Runway 03C at Detroit Metropolitan Wayne County Airport bound for Phoenix, Arizona, one segment of a domestic service originating at Saginaw, Michigan, with an ultimate destination of John Wayne Airport, Orange County in southern California. Only 14 seconds after becoming airborne, and while at an approximate height of 50ft (15m) above the ground, the aircraft struck, with its port (left) wing, a lamp standard located about 0.5 mile (0.8km) beyond the end of the runway.

With its undercarriage still in the process of retracting, the MD-82 then clipped other lamp standards and the roof of a building and rolled to the left in excess of 90° before it hit the ground, disintegrated and burst into flames, scattering wreckage along a road, and under a railroad and two highway overpasses. 156 people were killed in the disaster, including the aircraft's six crew members and two occupants of vehicles hit by the crashing airliner. The sole surviving passenger was a four-year-old girl travelling with her parents and brother. She suffered severe burns, a fractured skull and other impact-related trauma. Five other people on the ground were also injured, one seriously, and numerous vehicles, three on the road and the rest parked in a rental-car lot, destroyed.

Examination of the debris disclosed no evidence of a malfunction in the airliner's engines, flight controls or avionics that could have directly contributed to the accident. One significant find was made, however: its flaps and leading-edge slats were confirmed to be retracted at the time of the crash. This was further corroborated by the position of the cockpit flap-slat handle and by the digital flight data recorder (DFDR) read-out, which includes these items among its transcribed parameters.

Playback of the cockpit voice recorder (CVR) tape also revealed that the two-man flight crew neither called for nor carried out the taxi checklist, on which the extension of the flaps and slats is the first item. In accordance with Northwest Airline procedures, the first officer usually set them after the start of the taxi, but at around the time that this should have been done, the co-pilot of N321RC was receiving information regarding a change of take-off runway. There was speculation that by the time he finished copying this automatic terminal information service (ATIS) message, the MD-82 had progressed beyond the point where the extension would normally be completed, which may have misled him to believe that the task had been accomplished.

The stated policy of the airline is that the captain is supposed to initiate the check-list routine. The captain of Flight 255 did not ask for the after-start, taxi or before-take-off checks, relegating this responsibility to his first officer. These and other factors, including confusion over the location of a particular taxi-way despite the fact that the pilot had flown into this airport many times, led the US National Transportation Safety Board (NTSB) to conclude in its investigative report that the conduct of the crew did not conform to air carrier

ABOVE: Passengers in this MD-81 airliner crash on 27 December 1991, had a far better chance of survival than they would have had 20 years earlier. There was no fire in the SAS *Dana Viking* crash, even though the airliner broke into three and it was loaded with fuel. *PA News Photo Library*

standards, even though both pilots had gained a reputation for competence and professionalism from their peers. The omission of the taxi check-list was, in fact, regarded by the NTSB as the primary cause of the disaster.

The MD-82 is equipped with a sophisticated control aural warning system (CAWS), which has an important component designed to recognise the conditions that could precipitate a stall, such as an improper flap-slat configuration, and is activated by movement of the thrust levers. No such aural warning (consisting of a voice stating 'flaps' and/or 'slats') was transcribed by the cockpit voice recorder (CVR), which the NTSB attributed to a loss of electrical power to the system. This may have resulted from intentional action by the crew or maintenance personnel; from a transient overload; or because the circuit breaker did not allow the current to flow to the control aural warning system (CAWS) power supply and did not annunciate the condition by tripping. The power loss was considered the principal contributing factor in the crash.

The absence of extended flaps and slats would have severely limited the climb capability and increased the airliner's stalling speed. This accounted for its relatively long take-off ground run and the fact that N312RC assumed a higher-than-normal pitch angle after becoming airborne while gaining little altitude. The stick-shaker stall-warning system was heard on the cockpit voice recorder (CVR) tape to activate less than a second after lift-off. Once in the air the airliner began rocking laterally, which the crew attempted to control by deploying the spoilers. The 'Dutch roll' motions and corrective action further decreased the performance of the MD-82.

A section of the left (port) outer wing some 18ft (15.5m) long was torn off in the initial impact with the lamp standard, rupturing fuel tanks. Escaping fuel was then ingested into the

ABOVE: By the end of 1997 American Airlines had 260 MD-80 airliners listed in its large fleet, these included 234 MD-82s and 26 MD-83s. One of them, MD-82 N275AA seen in landing configuration during October 1996, was damaged on landing at Cleveland Hopkins International Airport, Ohio on 5 March 1997. MAP

airliner's No 1 power plant and ignited, this explaining the in-flight fire reported by some witnesses.

The accident occurred at twilight (20.45hrs); the weather at the time was fair, with a high overcast and scattered clouds down to 2,500ft (c750m), a visibility of around 5 miles (10km) and a 12-knot wind out of the west. Wind shear advisories had been broadcast shortly before the departure of Flight 255, although there was no evidence from available information, including the digital flight data recorder (DFDR) read-out, that such a condition in any way contributed to the crash. Nevertheless, the alert may have influenced the actions of the crew, even to the point of reducing their ability to escape from the stall. The captain, who was flying the aircraft, apparently increased its pitch angle after the stall warning, showing he sus-pected an encounter with wind shear; stall recovery procedures normally involve lowering the nose and extending the flaps, which in this case would probably have prevented the disaster.

Subsequently, all operators of the MD-80 series incorporat-ed a crew check-list procedure to ensure that the control aural warning system (CAWS) was functional prior to take-off. The US National Transportation Safety Board also recommended that the system's fail light be modified to compensate for its inability to annunciate in the event of a power loss.

In May 1991 a US federal court rejected Northwest Airlines' contention that McDonnell Douglas share responsi-bility for the accident, ruling that the carrier was liable for all damages resulting therefrom.

12 June 1988: MD-81 N1003G   Posadas, Argentina

Completed at Long Beach on 16 April 1981, it was delivered as N1003G to Austral Lineas Aereas at Buenos Aires, Argentina on 8 August 1981. On 12 June 1988 N1003G crashed on final approach to Posadas airport in Argentina during bad weather. There were 22 fatalities. The airliner was powered by two JT8D-209 turbofan engines and had completed 19,280 flying hours and accomplished 19,819 landings.

27 December 1991: MD-81 OY-KHO   Stockholm, Sweden

MD-81 *Dana Viking* was sixth of a batch of 12 ordered by SAS with deliveries late in 1990 and early 1991. OY-KHO first flew at Long Beach on 29 March 1991 and was delivered on 10 April. It was powered by two JT8D-217 turbofan engines. On Friday 27 December 1991 it was operating SAS flight SK751 out of Arlando, Stockholm to Bromma, Copenhagen with 123 passengers and six crew. Due to below freezing temperatures the flight had been delayed some 18 minutes whilst ice was removed from the airliner's wings, so it was 7.48am when the MD-81 finally took off from Arlando. Only three minutes after take-off Captain Stefan Rasmussen reported losing power on both engines at an altitude of 1,800ft (549m). In a brilliant 'controlled crash' landing (see photograph on page 105) in which the pilot slowed the airliner's flight by brushing the tops of fir trees the Danish pilot saved the lives of the 129 occupants. Total flying hours were 1,608 with 1,272 landings.

26 October 1993 MD-82 B-2103   Fuzhou, PRC

Completed at Long Beach on 8 August 1985, on 7 October 1985 the airplane was registered as B-2103 to the Civil Aviation Administration (CAA) of China and delivered on that date. On 1 May 1988 it was transferred to China Eastern Airlines based at Hongqlao International Airport, Shanghai and on 26 October 1993 the airliner was damaged beyond repair after over-running the runway at Fuzhou, Fujian Province, PRC. There were two fatalities and 79 survivors. The airliner was powered by two JT8D-217 turbofan engines and had complet-ed 18,718 flying hours and accomplished 11,942 landings.

30 November 1993: MD-82 B-28003   Taiwan

Completed at Long Beach during August 1991, it was delivered as B-28003 to Far Eastern Air Transport at Taipai, Taiwan, on 30 October 1991. On 30 November 1993 the MD-82 pilot experienced engine difficulties immediately after take-off from Kaohsiung, Taiwan. He returned to the airport and made a very hard landing. The undercarriage collapsed and the left (port) wing separated and the airliner hit a small building and was severely damaged. Happily, there were only nine minor injuries. The airliner was powered by two JT8D-217 turbofan engines and had completed 4,529 hours and accomplished 8,195 landings.

24 November 1993: MD-87 SE-DIB   Denmark

Delivered as SE-DIB *Varin Viking* to SAS in October 1988, on 24 November 1993 a fire broke out in the lavatory after landing at Copenhagen resulting in major damage to the airliner — although, fortunately, no injuries. Repaired, by the end of December 1996 this airliner had flown 18,573 hours and accomplished 12,766 landings. It is still in service with SAS and powered by two JT8D-217 turbofan engines.

13 December 1993: MD-82 B-2141   Urumqui, PRC

Constructed in China by the Shanghai Industrial Corporation, it was bought by China Northern Airlines on 31 December 1991. On 13 December 1993 it crash-landed in a field and caught fire while on final approach to Urumqui airport in fog. There were 12 fatalities and 90 survivors. The airliner was powered by two JT8D-217 turbofan engines and had flown 5,002 hours and accomplished 2,694 landings.

2 March 1994: MD-82 N18835   La Guardia, NYC, USA

On 2 March 1994 the airliner ran off the end of the runway during an aborted take-off at New York, La Guardia, during a snowstorm, coming to rest on a dike and a tidal mud flat. Some 19 seconds had elapsed between the time that N18835 actually accelerated through 60 knots indicated air speed (the first mark on the airspeed indicator) and the start of the rejected take-off.

The flight data recorder on recovery,confirmed that the pitot head system heat had not been selected 'on' by the flight crew. A build up of snow and/or ice in the pitot static system tubes and ports resulted in erroneous airspeed readings during the attempted take-off. Substantial deviation from check list procedures were recorded. There were 30 minor injuries and 86 uninjured.

The US National Transport Safety Board gave the possible cause of the accident to the failure of the flight crew to comply with check list procedures to turn on an operable pitot static heat system, resulting in ice and/or snow blockage of the pitot tubes that produced erroneous airspeed indications, and the flight crew's untimely response to anomalous airspeed indications with the consequent rejections of take-off at an actual speed of 5 knots above VI. (*NTSB Report AAR-95/01*)

N18835 was seen in a hangar at La Guardia in the process of being repaired returned to flight status with Continental Airlines and by the end of December 1996 had flown 30,887 hours and accomplished 14,527 landings. It was powered by two JT8D-217 turbofan engines.

6 September 1994: MD-83 SE-DPI   Palma, Majorca

This MD-83 made its first flight from Long Beach on 25 January 1988. Bought by SAS Leisure in 1991 it was on lease to Spanair when, on 6 September 1994, the airliner was damaged by an electrical fire at Palma, Majorca. The MD-83 was ferried back to Oslo for repairs and is still in service today. By the end of December 1996 it had flown a total of 23,485 hours and accomplished 10,866 landings.

3 November 1994: MD-83 F-GHED   Kajaani, Finland

Bought by Air Liberté and registered F-GHED, on 4 May 1990 F-GHED was leased to Air Liberté Tunisia. Damage was sustained when it touched down too far beyond the runway threshold at Kajaani airport, Finland, and veered off the runway.. It was thought the airliner would be written-off, but it is still listed as current and up to the end of December 1996 it had flown a total of 20,851 hours and accomplished 10,253 landings. It is powered by two JT8D-210 turbofan engines.

22 November 1994: MD-82 N954U   St Louis, MI, USA

Completed at Long Beach on 17 July 1987, it was delivered on 4 December 1987 to Polaris Aircraft Leasing Corporation and leased to TWA on 31 December 1987 with fleet no 9054. On 22 November 1994 N954U hit a wing of Cessna 441 N441KM whilst taxiing for take-off at St Louis International Airport, Missouri. The cabin roof and tail sheared off the Cessna killing both Cessna pilots. Damage to the MD-82 wing was repairable. The airliner is powered by two JT8D-217 turbofan engines; it is still in service with TWA and by the end of December 1996 had flown 27,867 hours and accomplished 14,310 landings.

November 1995: MD-83 N566AA   Hartford, CT, USA

This MD-83 was completed at Long Beach on 27 April 1987 and delivered to American on 15 June. During November 1995 it was badly damaged when it hit trees and landed short at Hartford, Connecticut. On 25 November 1995 it was ferried to Tulsa, Oklahoma for repairs which were expected to take several months. It is powered by two JT8D-219 turbofan engines. According to Long Beach and airline records this airliner is still in service and up to the end of December 1996 had flown 30,985 hours and accomplished 14,879 landings.

5 March 1997: MD-82 N275AA   Cleveland, OH, USA

Delivered to American on 13 November 1984, it was powered by two JT8D-217 turbofans and by the end of the 1996 had completed 37,345 flying hours. On 5 March 1997 it slid off the left hand side of Runway 5R on landing at Cleveland Hopkins International Airport, Ohio, after a flight from Dallas–Fort Worth.

The airliner sustained an undetermined amount of damage caused by the collapse of the right main undercarriage. Three of the 103 passengers reported minor injuries, but the remainder, plus the six crew were uninjured.

8 PRODUCTION HISTORY

Airlines and operations shown in the production listing are the first operators only of each airliner produced. This does not automatically confer ownership, as since the middle 1980s large fleets of airliners have been and are still currently being purchased from the manufacturer by specialist leasing companies such as the International Lease Finance Corporation (ILFC) Beverly Hills, California; Polaris Leasing of San Francisco and the huge Guinness Peat Aviation Group based in Shannon, Eire.

The partial production listing is by f/n (fuselage number) followed by the s/n or c/n (serial or constructors number) as this system is a more accurate method of recording the production on the line in the Long Beach factory. Some airliners were ordered but never built, often leaving a blank in the f/n and s/n. Here are a few examples.

Two MD-82s s/n 48064/5 were ordered by Air California but cancelled. Likewise, s/n 48160/1/2/3/4 for Midway Airlines and three MD-82s for Pacific Southwest

with s/n 49240/1/2 were also ordered and then cancelled. Muse Air ordered MD-82s and had the registrations allocated before the order was cancelled. These were N938MC s/n 49375; N939MC s/n 49376; N940MC s/n 49377; and N941MC s/n 49378. A single MD-83 s/n 49495 is unique in that it was ordered by Air 2000, the United Kingdom operator, but never built. This was followed by five for TWA, all MD-82s s/n 49496/7/8/9/500. These cancellations took place in the 1980s.

In 1993 a large batch of airplanes suffered not being built for a variety of reasons — though mostly financial. These included MD-88s f/n 2085 53424 N921DE and f/n 2087 s/n 53425 N922DE for Delta, followed by MD-82 s/n 53426. 53432/3/4 for LOT Polish Airlines, the last three being in fact MD-87s. Irish Aerospace ordered and cancelled MD-83 s/n 53427. Eight MD-83s were involved in a Shanghai Aviation Industrial Corporation order, these being s/n 53435/6/7/8/9/40/1/2.

Fuselage No	Serial No	Model	Registration	Operator	Delivery
909	48000	-81	N980DC	Douglas Aircraft Co	18/1079
917	48001	-81	N1002G	Douglas Aircraft Co	01/12/79
924	48015	-81	OE-LDP	Douglas Aircraft Co	29/02/80
				Austrian Airlines	16/05/81
938	48002	-81	HB-INC	Swissair	13/09/80
941	48016	-81	OE-LDR	Austrian Airlines	03/10/80
944	48003	-81	HB-IND	Swissair	26/10/80
946	48034	-81	N924PS	PSA	14/11/80
948	48024	-81	N10022	Austral Lineas Aereas	08/01/81
950	48004	-81	HB-INE	Swissair	21/11/80
952	48025	-81	N10027	Austral	08/01/81
953	48029	-81	JA8458	TDA	30/01/81
955	48035	-81	N925PS	PSA	31/03/81
957	48005	-81	HB-INF	Swissair	28/01/81
958	48017	-81	OE-LDS	Austrian Airlines	16/01/81
960	48026	-81	N10028	Musa Air Corporation	29/06/81
962	48030	-81	JA8459	TDA	05/03/81
962	48036	-81	N926PS	PSA	09/03/81
965	48037	-81	N927PS	PSA	08/01/81
966	48006	-81	HB-ING	Swissair	03/04/81
967	48044	-81	N809HA	Hawaiian Airlines	24/04/81
969	48031	-81	JA8460	TDA	17/04/81
970	48045	-81	N819HA	Hawaiian Airlines	04/05/81
971	48007	-81	HB-INH	Swissair	08/05/81
973	48027	-81	N475AC	Air California	15/05/81
974	48052	-81	N928PS	PSA	15/05/81
975	48051	-81	N829HA	Hawaiian Airlines	10/06/81
977	48046	-81	YU-AJZ	Inex Adria Aviopromet	10/06/81

Fuselage No	Serial No	Model	Registration	Operator	Delivery
978	48032	-81	JA8461	TDA	10/04/81
979	48028	-81	N476AC	Air California	08/06/81
981	48008	-81	HB-INI	Swissair	02/07/81
983	48049	-81	N10029	Muse Air	02/07/81
985	48009	-81	HB-INK	Swissair	20/06/81
986	48053	-81	N929PS	PSA	10/07/81
988	48033	-81	JA8462	TDA	29/07/81
989	48050	-81	N1003G	Austral	08/08/81
991	48058	-81	N8839HA	Hawaiian Airlines	20/07/81
992	48010	-81	HB-INL	Swissair	24/07/81
994	48011	-81	HB-INM	Swissair	05/08/81
995	48018	-81	OE-LDT	Austrian Airlines	25/07/81
996	48054	-82	N301RC	Republic Airlines	05/08/81
997	48012	-81	HB-INN	Swissair	29/08/91
998	48047	-82	YU-ANA	Inex Adria	11/08/81
999	48070	-81	JA8468	TDA	09/11/81
1000	48013	-81	HB-INO	Swissair	04/09/81
1001	48019	-81	OE-LDU	Austrian Airlines	05/09/81
1002	48038	-81	N930PS	PSA	10/09/81
1003	48039	-81	N931PS	PSA	10/09/81
1004	48071	-81	JA8469	TDA	18/12/81
1005	48048	-82	YU-ANB	Inex Adria	19/09/81
1006	48040	-81	N932PS	PSA	10/09/81
1007	48055	-82	N302RC	Republic Airlines	05/09/81
1008	48041	-81	N933PS	PSA	28/09/81
1009	48042	-81	N934PS	PSA	28/09/81
1010	48043	-81	N935PS	PSA	08/10/81
1011	48072	-81	JA8470	TDA	25/02/81
1012	48056	-82	N930MC	Muse Air	07/05/81
1013	48014	-81	HB-INP	Swissair	30/10/81
1015	48062	-82	N477AC	Air California	15/10/81
1016	48079	-82	N779JA	Jet America Airlines	13/11/81
1018	48073	-81	N849HA	Hawaiian Airlines	25/11/81
1019	48066	-82	N479AC	Air California	15/10/81
1020	48063	-82	N478AC	Air California	21/10/81
1022	48080	-82	N778JA	Jet America Airlines	13/11/81
1023	48057	-82	N931MC	Muse Air	07/05/82
1025	49100	-81	HB-INA	Swissair	12/12/81
1026	48074	-81	N859HA	Hawaiian Airlines	11/12/81
1028	48067	-82	N1003X	Aeromexico	22/12/81
1029	48086	-82	N307RC	Republic Airlines	21/12/81
1031	48068	-82	N1003Y	Aeromexico	22/12/81
1032	48069	-82	N1003Z	Aeromexico	27/12/81
1034	48092	-81	N936PS	PSA	17/12/81
1035	48087	-82	YU-ANC	Inex Adria	02/04/82
1037	48088	-82	N309RC	Republic Airlines	02/12/82
1038	48089	-82	N311RC	Republic Airlines	02/12/82
1040	48090	-82	N312RC	Republic Airlines	08/12/82
1041	48091	-82	N1004G	Republic Airlines	26/04/83
1043	48083	-82	N10033	Aeromexico	26/02/82
1045	48020	-81	OE-LDV	Austrian Airlines	12/02/82
1047	48059	-81	LE-LDW	Austrian Airlines	20/02/82
1049	48093	-81	N937PS	PSA	22/03/82

Fuselage No	Serial No	Model	Registration	Operator	Delivery
1051	49101	-81	HB-INB	Swissair	17/03/82
1053	48094	-81	N938PS	PSA	07/04/82
1055	48095	-82	N940PS	PSA	23/04/82
1057	48096	-82	N941PS	PSA	20/05/82
1059	48097	-82	N942PS	PSA	20/05/82
1060	48098	-82	N943PS	PSA	27/05/82
1061	49116	-82	N9801F	Frontier Airlines	22/04/82
1062	49110	-82	N1004L	Republic Airlines	26/08/83
1063	49117	-82	N9802F	Frontier Airlines	04/05/82
1064	49111	-82	N781JA	Jet America Airlines	09/12/83
1065	49118	-82	N9803F	Frontier Airlines	13/05/82
1066	49114	-82	N9804F	Frontier Airlines	03/12/82
1067	48099	-81	N939PS	PSA	17/06/82
1068	49112	-82	N480AC	Air California	28/05/82
1069	49113	-82	N481AC	Air California	22/06/82
1070	49119	-82	N944PS	PSA	15/07/82
1071	49120	-81	N932MC	Muse Air	28/09/82
1072	49121	-81	N933MC	Muse Air	28/09/82
1073	49122	-81	N934MC	Muse Air	14/12/82
1074	49125	-81	N935MC	Muse Air	29/11/82
1075	49123	-82	PJ-SEF	ALM-Antillean Airways	04/10/82
1076	49102	-82	N9805F	Frontier Airlines	24/11/82
1077	49124	-82	J-SEG	ALM	04/10/82
1078	48021	-81	OE-LDX	Austrian Airlines	28/02/83
1079	48022	-82	PH-MCD	Martinair Holland	28/03/83
1080	49126	-82	N780JA	Jet America Airlines	11/03/83
1082	49127	-82	N801NY	New York Air	02/09/83
1083	49103	-82	YV158C	VIASA	30/12/82
1085	49104	-82	YV159C	VIASA	30/12/82
1086	49149	-82	N505MD	Douglas Aircraft Co	
			PP-OJM	Cruzeiro do Sul	08/12/82
1087	49150	-82	OH-LMN	Finnair	11/03/83
1088	49151	-82	OH-LMO	Finnair	25/03/83
1089	49152	-82	OH-LMP	Finnair	29/04/83
1090	49138	-82	N945PS	PSA	18/04/83
1091	49139	-82	N946PS	PSA	12/05/83
1092	49140	-82	B2101	CAAC	12/12/83
1093	49141	-82	B2102	CAAC	12/12/83
1094	49142	-82	N947PS	PSA	17/10/83
1095	49143	-82	N948PS	PSA	17/12/82
1096	49144	-82	PH-MBZ	Martinair Holland	15/02/83
1097	49145	-82	N203AA	American Airlines	10/05/83
1098	49166	-82	N901TW	TWA-Trans World Airlines	18/04/83
1099	49167	-82	N216AA	American Airlines	10/05/83
1100	49168	-82	N218AA	American Airlines	04/05/83
1101	49153	-82	N902TW	TWA	24/05/83
1102	49154	-82	N903TW	TWA	12/05/83
1103	49155	-82	N205AA	American Airlines	06/06/83
1104	49156	-82	N904TW	TWA	24/05/83
1105	49157	-82	N905TW	TWA	27/05/83
1106	49158	-82	N207AA	American Airlines	07/06/83
1107	49159	-82	N208AA	American Airlines	27/06/83
1108	49160	-82	N906TW	TWA	23/06/83

Fuselage No	Serial No	Model	Registration	Operator	Delivery
1109	49161	-82	N210AA	American Airlines	28/06/83
1110	49162	-82	N214AA	American Airlines	29/07/83
1111	49163	-82	N215AA	American Airlines	01/08/83
1112	49171	-82	N219AA	American Airlines	02/08/83
1113	49172	-82	N221AA	American Airlines	17/08/83
1113	49173	-82	N223AA	American Airlines	02/09/83
1115	49174	-82	N224AA	American Airlines	29/08/83
1116	49175	-82	N225AA	American Airlines	08/09/83
1117	49165	-82	N907TW	TWA	02/09/83
1118	49169	-82	N908TW	TWA	22/09/83
1119	49170	-82	N909TW	TWA	13/10/83
1120	49176	-82	N226AA	American Airlines	26/10/83
1121	49177	-82	N227AA	American Airlines	28/10/83
1122	49178	-82	N228AA	American Airlines	01/11/83
1123	49179	-82	N232AA	American Airlines	03/11/83
1124	49180	-82	N233AA	American Airlines	30/11/83
1125	49181	-82	N234AA	American Airlines	06/12/83
1126	49192	-82	I-DAWA	Alitalia	16/12/83
1127	49193	-82	I-DAWE	Alitalia	16/12/83
1128	49182	-82	N-911TW	TWA	09/12/83
1129	49183	-82	N912TW	TWA	20/12/83
1130	49194	-82	I-DAWI	Alitalia	24/02/84
1131	49184	-82	N913TW	TWA	23/03/84
1132	49185	-82	N914TW	TWA	13/04/84
1133	49186	-82	N915TW	TWA	19/04/84
1134	49187	-82	N916TW	TWA	25/04/84
1135	49115	-82	OE-LDY	Austrian Airlines	04/05/84
1136	49195	-82	I-DAWO	Alitalia	11/05/84
1137	49196	-82	I-DAWU	Alitalia	20/05/84
1138	49197	-82	I-DAWB	Alitalia	27/05/84
1139	49222	-82	N802NY	New York Air	25/06/84
1140	49229	-82	N803NY	New York Air	21/06/84
1141	49230	-82	N95OU	American Airlines	19/06/84
1142	49198	-82	I-DWAC	Alitalia	26/06/84
1143	49199	-82	I-DAWD	Alitalia	30/06/84
1144	49237	-82	N949PS	PSA	30/06/84
1145	49245	-82	N951U	American Airlines	20/06/84
1146	49246	-82	N804NY	New York Air	06/08/84
1147	49200	-82	I-DAWF	Alitalia	24/07/84
1148	49201	-82	I-DAWG	Alitalia	30/07/84
1149	49249	-82	N805NY	New York Air	14/08/84
1150	49260	-82	N806NY	New York Air	22/08/84
1151	49247	-82	HB-IKK	Alisarda	20/09/84
1152	49248	-82	HB-IKL	Alisarda	27/09/84
1153	49261	-82	N807NY	New York Air	05/09/84
1154	49251	-82	N236AA	American Airlines	06/09/84
1155	49253	-82	N237AA	American Airlines	14/09/84
1156	49254	-82	N241AA	American Airlines	11/09/84
1157	49255	-82	N242AA	American Airlines	17/09/84
1158	49256	-82	N244AA	American Airlines	21/09/84
1159	49262	-82	N808NY	New York Air	15/11/84
1160	49257	-82	N245AA	American Airlines	02/10/84
1161	49258	-82	N246AA	American Airlines	09/10/84

Fuselage No	Serial No	Model	Registration	Operator	Delivery
1162	49259	-82	N248AA	American Airlines	15/10/84
1163	49263	-82	N809NY	New York Air	15/11/84
1164	49269	-82	N249AA	American Airlines	26/10/84
1165	49270	-82	N251AA	American Airlines	31/10/84
1166	49271	-82	N274AA	American Airlines	07/11/84
1167	49272	-82	N275AA	American Airlines	13/11/84
1168	49273	-82	N276AA	American Airlines	20/11/84
1169	49252	-82	OH-LMS	Finnair	19/10/84
1170	49202	-82	I-DAWH	Alitalia	30/11/84
1171	49264	-82	N810NY	New York Air	20/12/84
1172	49188	-82	XA-AMO	Aeromexico	17/12/84
1173	49189	-82	XA-AMP	Aeromexico	20/12/84
1174	49203	-82	I-DAWJ	ATI	18/12/84
1175	49286	-82	N253AA	American Airlines	04/01/85
1176	49287	-82	N255AA	American Airlines	15/01/84
1177	49231	-82	N930AS	Alaska Airlines	29/03/85
1178	49232	-82	N931AS	Alaska Airlines	20/02/85
1179	49204	-82	I-DAWL	Alitalia	19/02/85
1180	49190	-82	XA-AMQ	Aeromexico	10/02/85
1181	49277	-82	HB-INR	Balair	01/02/85
1182	49164	-81	OE-LDZ	Austrian Airlines	15/02/85
1183	49278	-81	LE-LMA	Austrian Airlines	27/02/85
1184	49205	-82	I-DAWM	Alitalia	27/02/85
1185	49265	-82	N811NY	New York Air	29/03/85
1186	49250	-82	N812NY	New York Air	04/04/85
1187	49288	-82	N258AA	American Airlines	08/03/85
1188	49206	-82	I-DAWP	Alitalia	15/03/85
1189	49207	-82	I-DAWO	Alitalia	20/03/85
1190	49208	-82	I-DAWR	Alitalia	25/03/85
1191	49209	-82	I-DAWS	Alitalia	02/04/85
1192	49210	-82	I-DAWT	ATI	08/04/85
1193	49289	-82	N259AA	American Airlines	08/04/85
1194	49280	-81	JA8496	TDA	09/04/85
1195	49290	-82	N262AA	American Airlines	19/04/85
1196	49366	-82	N917TW	TWA	23/04/85
1197	49367	-82	N918TW	TWA	25/04/85
1198	49368	-82	N919TW	TWA	02/05/85
1199	49369	-82	N920TW	TWA	08/05/85
1200	49281	-81	JA8497	TDA	20/05/85
1201	49373	-82	HL7272	Korean Air Lines	10/08/85
1202	49211	-82	I-DAWV	ATI	24/05/85
1203	49233	-82	N932AS	Alaska Airlines	14/06/85
1204	49234	-82	N933AS	Alaska Airlines	28/06/85
1205	49379	-82	YU-ANG	Inex Adria	08/06/85
1206	49370	-82	N816NY	New York Air	25/06/85
1207	49371	-82	N817NY	New York Air	28/06/85
1208	49374	-82	HL7273	Korean Air Lines	21/08/85
1209	49284	-83	OH-LMR	Finnair	26/06/85
1210	49291	-82	N266AA	American Airlines	02/07/85
1211	49292	-82	N269AA	American Airlines	10/07/85
1212	49293	-82	N271AA	American Airlines	16/07/85
1213	49294	-82	N278AA	American Airlines	17/07/85
1214	49295	-82	N279AA	American Airlines	25/07/85

Fuselage No	Serial No	Model	Registration	Operator	Delivery
1215	49296	-82	N283AA	American Airlines	29/07/85
1216	49297	-82	N285AA	American Airlines	03/08/85
1217	49298	-82	N286AA	American Airlines	06/08/85
1218	49299	-82	N287AA	American Airlines	13/08/85
1219	49300	-82	N288AA	American Airlines	16/08/85
1220	49301	-82	N289AA	American Airlines	22/08/85
1221	49302	-82	N290AA	American Airlines	27/08/85
1222	49303	-82	N291AA	American Airlines	03/09/85
1223	49304	-82	N292AA	American Airlines	06/09/85
1224	49355	-82	B2103	CAAC	07/10/85
1225	49380	-81	OY-KGT	SAS - Scandinavian Airlines System	10/10/85
1226	49305	-82	N293AA	American Airlines	23/09/85
1227	49306	-82	N294AA	American Airlines	25/09/85
1228	49307	-82	N295AA	American Airlines	02/10/85
1229	49308	-82	N296AA	American Airlines	07/10/85
1230	49279	-81	OE-LMB	Austrian Airlines	20/10/85
1231	49381	-81	OY-KGZ	SAS	20/10/85
1232	49382	-81	LN-RLE	SAS	26/10/85
1233	49212	-82	I-DAWW	ATI	04/11/85
1234	49235	-83	N934AS	Alaska Airlines	16/11/85
1235	49236	-83	N935AS	Alaska Airlines	10/12/85
1236	49383	-82	LN-RLF	SAS	17/11/85
1237	49384	-82	SE-DFS	SAS	02/12/85
1238	49266	-82	N952U	Ozark Air Lines	27/11/85
1239	49267	-82	N953U	Ozark Air Lines	04/12/85
1240	49425	-82	B2104	CAAC	28/11/85
1241	49428	-82	B2105	CAAC	26/12/85
1242	49429	-82	N951PS	PSA	25/04/86
1243	49213	-82	I-DAWY	ATI	18/12/85
1244	49385	-82	SE-DFT	SAS	20/12/85
1245	49214	-82	I-DAWZ	ATI	18/12/85
1246	49309	-82	N297AA	American Airlines	10/01/86
1247	49310	-82	N298AA	American Airlines	13/01/86
1248	49311	-82	N400AA	American Airlines	17/01/86
1249	49312	-82	N70401	American Airlines	24/01/86
1250	49356	-81	HB-INS	Swissair	25/01/86
1251	49357	-81	HB-INT	Swissair	14/02/86
1252	49372	-81	OE-LMC	Austrian Airlines	28/02/86
1253	49215	-82	I-DAVA	ATI	18/02/86
1254	49420	-81	OY-KGY	SAS	18/02/86
1255	49313	-82	N402AA	American Airlines	28/02/86
1256	49314	-82	N403AA	American Airlines	24/02/86
1257	49315	-82	N70404	American Airlines	04/03/86
1258	49316	-82	N405AA	American Airlines	07/03/86
1259	49317	-82	N406AA	American Airlines	11/03/86
1260	49415	-82	N2106	SAIC 1/CAAC	31/07/87
1261	49402	-83	D-ALLD	Aero Lloyd	25/03/86
1262	49216	-82	I-DAVB	Alitalia	20/03/86
1263	49421	-82	SE-DFU	SAS	21/03/86
1264	49422	-81	SE-DFV	SAS	26/03/86
1265	49318	-82	N407AA	American Airlines	04/04/86
1266	49319	-82	N408AA	American Airlines	09/04/86

Fuselage No	Serial No	Model	Registration	Operator	Delivery
1267	49320	-82	N409AA	American Airlines	11/04/86
1268	49217	-82	I-DAVC	ATI	29/04/86
1269	49390	-83	9Y-THN	BWIA International	25/04/86
1270	49391	-82	EI-BTA	Frontier Airlines	29/04/86
1271	49416	-82	HL7275	Korean Air Lines	14/05/86
1272	49392	-82	EI-BTB	Frontier Airlines	01/05/86
1273	49321	-82	N410AA	American Airlines	09/05/86
1274	49218	-82	I-DAVD	ATI	21/05/86
1275	49363	-83	N936AS	Alaska Airlines	29/05/86
1276	49364	-83	N937AS	Alaska Airlines	28/05/96
1277	49365	-83	N938AS	Alaska Airlines	03/06/86
1278	49417	-82	HL7276	Korean Air Lines	01/06/86
1279	49393	-82	EI-BTC	Frontier Airlines	02/06/86
1280	49322	-82	N411AA	American Airlines	06/06/86
1281	49323	-82	N412AA	American Airlines	24/06/86
1282	49282	-81	JA8498	TDA	20/06/86
1283	49423	-82	LN-RLG	SAS	27/06/86
1284	49424	-82	SE-DFX	SAS	20/06/86
1285	49394	-82	EI-BTD	Frontier Airlines	25/06/86
1286	49395	-83	YV-36C	LAV	30/06/86
1287	49386	-82	N784JA	Jet America Airlines	02/12/86
1288	49387	-82	N785JA	Jet America Airlines	02/12/86
1289	49324	-82	N413AA	American Airlines	14/07/86
1290	49325	-82	N33414	American Airlines	18/07/86
1291	49443	-82	N952PS	PSA	28/07/86
1292	49501	-82	B2107	SAIC 2/CAAC	17/12/86
1293	49478	-82	N818NY	New York Air	08/08/86
1294	49358	-81	HB-INU	Swissair	28/07/86
1295	49326	-82	N415AA	American Airlines	05/08/86
1296	49327	-82	N416AA	American Airlines	08/08/86
1297	49479	-82	N819NY	New York Air	15/08/86
1298	49480	-82	N820NY	New York Air	29/08/86
1299	49283	-81	JA8499	TDA	13/09/86
1300	49502	-82	B2108	SAIC 3/CAAC	13/04/88
1301	49328	-82	N417AA	American Airlines	22/08/86
1302	49329	-82	N418AA	American Airlines	28/08/86
1303	49436	-81	OY-KHC	SAS	08/09/86
1304	49440	-82	YU-ANO	Adria Airways	10/09/86
1305	49396	-83	SE-DHB	Transwede Airways	24/09/86
1306	49331	-82	N419AA	American Airways	12/09/86
1307	49332	-82	N420AA	American Airlines	10/09/86
1308	49481	-82	N72821	Continental Airlines	30/09/86
1309	49482	-82	N72822	Continental Airlines	03/10/86
1310	49219	-82	I-DAVF	ATI	09/10/86
1311	49333	-82	N77421	American Airlines	07/10/86
1312	49334	-82	N422AA	American Airlines	10/10/86
1313	49448	-83	9Y-THQ	BWIA International	17/10/86
1314	49483	-82	N76823	Continental Airlines	22/10/86
1315	49484	-82	N72824	Continental Airlines	04/11/86
1316	49485	-82	N72825	Continental Airlines	14/11/86
1317	49486	-82	N69826	Continental Airlines	25/11/86
1318	49439	-82	N18835	Continental Airlines	19/12/86
1319	49220	-82	I-DAVG	ATI	19/11/86

Fuselage No	Serial No	Model	Registration	Operator	Delivery
1320	49335	-82	N423AA	American Airlines	03/11/86
1321	49336	-82	N424AA	American Airlines	05/1//86
1322	49441	-82	N35836	Continental Airlines	08/12/86
1323	49444	-82	N936MC	Transtar Airlines	12/12/86
1324	49450	-82	N937MC	Transtar Airlines	12/12/86
1325	49337	-82	N70425	American Airlines	25/11/86
1326	49388	-87	N87MD	Douglas Aircraft Co	04/12/86
1327	49338	-82	N426AA	American Airlines	26/11/86
1328	49339	-82	N427AA	American Airlines	05/12/86
1329	49349	-82	N428AA	American Airlines	08/12/86
1330	49221	-82	I-DAVH	ATI	30/12/86
1331	49397	-83	SE-DHC	Transwede Airlines	16/02/87
1332	49398	-83	G-PATA	Paramount Airways	24/07/87
1333	49389	-87	SE-DHG	Douglas Aircraft Co	13/01/87
				Transwede Airways	04/08/88
1334	49430	-82	I-DAVI	Alitalia	30/12/86
1335	49487	-82	N77827	Continental Airlines	30/12/86
1336	49341	-82	N429AA	American Airlines	23/12/86
1337	49342	-82	N430AA	American Airlines	06/01/87
1338	49632	-82	N901DL	Delta Air Lines	09/03/87
1339	49343	-82	N431AA	American Airlines	26/05/87
1340	49525	-83	N938MC	Transtar Airlines	25/03/87
1341	49533	-82	N902DL	Delta Air Lines	12/03/87
1342	49526	-83	N939MC	Transtar Airlines	12/03/87
1343	49399	-83	F-GGMA	Minerve	18/03/87
1344	49534	-82	N903DL	Delta Air Lines	18/03/87
1345	49437	-82	LN-RLR	SAS	06/03/87
1346	49503	-82	B2109	SAIC 4/China Eastern	16/07/88
1347	49535	-82	N904DL	Delta Air Lines	28/03/87
1348	49536	-82	N905DL	Delta Air Lines	01/04/87
1349	49359	-81	HB-INV	Swissair	18/03/87
1350	49488	-82	N71828	Continental Airlines	02/04/87
1351	49489	-82	N72829	Continental Airlines	10/04/87
1352	49490	-82	N72830	Continental Airlines	10/04/87
1353	49438	-81	SE-DFY	SAS	10/04/87
1354	49449	-83	D-ALLE	Aero Lloyd	28/03/87
1355	49537	-82	N906DL	Delta Air Lines	24/04/87
1356	49400	-83	G-PATB	Paramount Airways	24/07/87
1357	49401	-83	EC-ECN	Canafrica Transportes Aereos	29/04/87
1358	49442	-83	EC-ECO	Canafrica	28/04/87
1359	49461	-81	JA8260	TDA	16/05/87
1360	49491	-82	N14831	Continental Airlines	05/05/86
1361	49492	-82	N85832	Continental Airlines	15/05/87
1362	49531	-82	I-SMEG	Alisarda	21/05/87
1363	49504	-82	B2120	SAIC 5/China Eastern	01/11/88
1364	49493	-82	N18833	Continental Airlines	19/05/87
1365	49538	-82	N907DL	Delta Air Lines	21/05/87
1366	49639	-82	N908DL	Delta Air Lines	24/05/87
1367	49567	-83	YV-38C	LAV	20/05/87
1368	49494	-82	N10834	Continental Airlines	29/05/87
1369	49580	-82	N14840	Continental Airlines	05/06/87
1370	49344	-83	N562AA	American Airlines	03/06/87
1371	49345	-83	N563AA	American Airlines	05/06/87

Fuselage No	Serial No	Model	Registration	Operator	Delivery
1372	49346	-83	N564AA	American Airlines	08/06/97
1373	49347	-83	N565AA	American Airlines	11/06/87
1374	49348	-83	N566AA	American Airlines	15/06/87
1375	49349	-83	N568AA	American Airlines	16/06/87
1376	49350	-82	N432AA	American Airlines	16/06/87
1377	49431	-82	I-DAVJ	Alitalia	23/06/87
1378	49432	-82	I-DAVK	Alitalia	23/06/87
1379	49554	-81	LM-RMA	SAS	07/07/87
1380	49568	-83	9Y-THR	BSWIA International	29/06/87
1381	49505	-82	B2121	SAIC 6/China Northern	15/12/88
1382	49527	-83	N931TW	TWA	10/07/87
1383	49528	-83	N9302B	TWA	16/07/87
1384	49581	-82	N15841	Continental Airlines	21/07/87
1385	49351	-83	N569AA	American Airlines	13/07/87
1386	49352	-83	N570AA	American Airlines	16/07/87
1387	49353	-83	N571AA	American Airlines	20/07/87
1388	49451	-82	N433AA	American Airlines	22/07/87
1389	49452	-82	N434AA	American Airlines	24/07/87
1390	49453	-82	N435AA	American Airlines	29/07/87
1391	49454	-82	N436AA	American Airlines	31/07/87
1392	49455	-82	N437AA	American Airlines	05/08/87
1393	49456	-82	N438AA	American Airlines	07/08/87
1394	49418	-82	HL7282	Korean Air Lines	18/08/87
1395	49540	-88	N909DL	Douglas Aircraft Co	20/08/87
				Delta Air Lines	29/12/87
1396	49529	-83	N9303K	TWA	03/09/87
1397	49530	-83	N9304C	TWA	09/09/87
1398	49457	-82	N439AA	American Airlines	25/08/87
1399	49426	-82	N954U	TWA	04/12/87
1400	49506	-82	B2122	SAIC 7/China Northern	06/03/89
1401	49427	-82	N955U	TWA	04/12/87
1402	49555	-82	OY-KHD	SAS	04/09/87
1403	49419	-82	HL7283	Korean Air Lines	09/09/87
1404	49403	-87	OH-LMA	Finnair	18/09/87
1405	49569	-82	HB-INW	Balair	18/09/87
1406	49458	-83	N572AA	American Airlines	18/09/87
1407	49459	-82	N440AA	American Airlines	21/09/87
1408	49460	-82	N441AA	American Airlines	23/09/87
1409	49468	-82	N442AA	American Airlines	28/09/87
1410	49469	-82	N443AA	American Airlines	30/09/87
1411	49582	-82	N57837	Continental Airlines	07/10/87
1412	49411	-87	OE-LMK	Austrian Airlines	27/11/87
1413	49574	-83	EC-EFU	LAC	19/10/87
1414	49575	-83	EC-EFJ	Spantax Lineas Aereas	29/10/87
1415	49556	-83	SE-DFP	SAS	19/12/87
1416	49441	-88	N910DL	Delta Air Lines	19/12/87
1417	49470	-82	N73444	American Airlines	26/10/87
1418	49471	-82	N445AA	American Airlines	28/10/87
1419	49634	-82	N34838	Continental Airlines	24/11/87
1420	49635	-82	N14839	Continental Airlines	24/11/87
1421	49642	-83	SE-DHF	Transwede Airlines	21/02/88
1422	49576	-83	EC-EFK	Spantax	23/11/87
1423	49643	-83	G-BNSA	BIA-British Island Airways	31/12/87

Fuselage No	Serial No	Model	Registration	Operator	Delivery
1424	49412	-87	OE-LML	Austrian Airlines	23/12/87
1425	49507	-82	B2123	SAIC8/China Eastern	31/05/89
1526	49472	-82	N466AA	American Airlines	20/11/87
1427	49473	-82	N447AA	American Airlines	24/11/87
1428	49433	-82	I-DAVL	ATI	21/01/88
1429	49662	-83	G-PATC	Paramount Airways	25/02/88
1430	40404	-87	OH-LMB	Finnair	08/01/88
1431	49474	-82	N448AA	American Airlines	11/12/87
1432	49475	-82	N449AA	American Airlines	16/12/87
1433	49542	-88	N911DL	Delta Air Lines	29/12/87
1434	49443	-88	N912DL	Delta Air Lines	30/12/87
1435	49602	-83	D-ALLF	Aero Lloyd	21/12/87
1436	49557	-83	LN-RMB	SAS	???????
1437	49663	-83	G-PATD	Paramount Airways	???????
1438	49659	-83	YV-39C	LAV	27/02/88
1439	49476	-82	N450AA	American Airlines	03/02/88
1440	49570	-81	HB-INX	Swissair	25/02/88
1441	49477	-82	N451AA	American Airlines	02/02/88
1442	49603	-81	SE-DIA	SAS	26/04/88
1443	49544	-88	N913DL	Delta Air Lines	21/02/88
1444	49545	-88	N914DL	Delta Air Lines	25/02/88
1445	49660	-82	EI-BTX	Unifly Express	10/03/88
1446	49434	-82	I-DAVM	Alitalia	01/03/88
1447	49546	-88	N915DL	Delta Air Lines	07/03/88
1448	49591	-88	N916DL	Delta Air Lines	31/03/88
1449	49508	-82	B2124	SAIC 9/China Northern	31/????
1450	49553	-82	N452AA	American Airlines	26/????
1451	49558	-82	N453AA	American Airlines	02/03/88
1452	49661	-82	SU-DAK	ZAS Airline of Egypt	10/03/88
1453	49670	-87	D0ALLG	Aero Lloyd	15/03/88
1454	49577	-83	EC-EHT	Spanair	25/03/88
1455	49578	-83	SE-DHD	Transwede Airways	16/03/88
1456	49604	-82	OY-KHE	SAS	21/04/88
1457	49585	-87	HB-IUA	CTA	04/04/88
1458	49571	-81	EB-INY	Swissair	26/03/88
1459	49657	-83	N939AS	Alaska Airlines	08/04/89
1460	49559	-82	N454AA	American Airlines	31/03/88
1461	49658	-83	G-BNSB	BIA	12/????
1462	49560	-82	N455AA	American Airlines	06/????
1463	49671	-87	D-ALLH	Aero Lloyd	15/04/88
1464	49617	-83	F-GGMB	Minerve	29/04/88
1465	49579	-83	EC-EIG	Spanair	25/04/88
1466	49667	-82	EI-BTY	Unifly Express	15/05/88
1467	49668	-82	EC-EIK	Oasis International Airlines	26/05/88
1468	49572	-81	HB-INZ	Swissair	07/05/88
1469	49573	-88	N917DL	Delta Air Lines	25/05/88
1470	49583	-88	N918DL	Delta Air Lines	14/05/88
1471	49584	-88	N919DL	Delta Air Lines	19/05/88
1472	49586	-87	HB-IUB	CTA	14/05/88
1473	49644	-88	N920DL	Delta Air Lines	06/06/88
1474	49561	-82	N456AA	American Airlines	24/05/88
1475	49562	-82	N457AA	American Airlines	20/????
1476	49464	-87	JA8279	Japan Air System	02/06/88

Fuselage No	Serial No	Model	Registration	Operator	Delivery
1477	49462	-81	JA8261	Japan Air System	13/06/88
1478	49701	-82	N14846	TWA	17/06/88
1479	49702	-82	N14847	TWA	17/06/88
1480	49645	-88	N921DL	Delta Air Lines	08/06/88
1481	49646	-88	N922DL	Delta Air Lines	15/06/88
1482	49509	-82	B2125	SAIC 10/China Eastern	08/11/89
1483	49619	-83	EI-BTU	Unifly Express	30/06/88
1484	49620	-83	EI-BTV	Unifly Express	01/07/88
1485	49563	-82	N458AA	American Airlines	17/06/88
1486	49564	-82	N459AA	American Airlines	21/06/88
1487	49707	-83	F-GFZB	Air Libert=8E	26/07/88
1488	49463	-81	JA8262	Japan Air System	21/07/88
1489	49703	-82	N958U	TWA	06/07/88
1490	49704	-82	N959U	TWA	06/07/88
1491	49705	-88	N923DL	Delta Air Lines	15/07/88
1492	49711	-88	N924DL	Delta Air Lines	27/07/88
1493	49669	-82	I-SMEV	Alisarda	19/07/88
1494	49672	-83	EC-EJQ	Spanair	27/07/88
1495	49621	-83	EC-EJU	Spanair	29/07/88
1496	49565	-82	N460AA	American Airlines	26/07/88
1497	49566	-82	N461AA	American Airlines	02/08/88
1498	49622	-83	EC-EJZ	LAC-Lineas Aereas Canarias	16/08/88
1499	49623	-83	SE-DHN	Transwede Airlines	19/08/88
1500	49712	-88	N925DL	Delta Air Lines	16/08/88
1501	49605	-87	SE-DIB	SAS	26/10/88
1502	49624	-83	EC-EKM	Oasis International	24/08/88
1503	49625	-83	OH-LMG	Finnair	26/08/88
1504	49435	-82	I-DAVN	ATI	05/10/88
1505	49592	-82	N462AA	American Airlines	30/08/88
1506	49593	-82	N463AA	American Airlines	31/08/88
1507	49594	-82	N464AA	American Airlines	12/09/88
1508	49673	-87		Douglas Aircraft Co	07/09/88
1509	49595	-82	N465AA	American Airlines	14/09/88
1510	49596	-82	N466AA	American Airlines	19/09/88
1511	49597	-82	N467AA	American Airlines	22/09/88
1512	49607	-87	SE-DIC	SAS	30/09/88
1513	49598	-82	N468AA	American Airlines	28/09/88
1514	49510	-82	B2126	SAIC 11/China Northern	12/89
1515	49599	-82	N469AA	American Airlines	27/09/88
1516	49600	-82	N470AA	American Airlines	04/10/88
1517	49609	-87	OY-KHF	SAS	07/10/88
1518	49601	-82	N471AA	American Airlines	07/10/88
1519	49613	-81	OY-KHG	SAS	14/10/88
1520	49647	-82	N472AA	American Airlines	12/10/88
1521	49648	-82	N473AA	American Airlines	17/10/88
1522	49611	-87	LN-RMG	SAS	05/11/88
1523	49712	-88	N926DL	Delta Air Lines	28/10/88
1524	49714	-88	N927DL	Delta Air Lines	01/11/88
1525	49405	-87	OH-LMC	Finnair	24/10/88
1526	49649	-82	N474AA	American Airlines	25/10/88
1527	49650	-82	N475AA	American Airlines	02/11/88
1528	49651	-82	N476AA	American Airlines	28/10/88
1529	49652	-82	N477AA	American Airlines	07/11/88

Fuselage No	Serial No	Model	Registration	Operator	Delivery
1530	49715	-88	N928DL	Delta Air Lines	10/11/88
1531	49716	-88	N929DL	Delta Air Lines	17/11/88
1532	49717	-88	N930DL	Delta Air Lines	18/11/88
1533	49718	-88	N931DL	Delta Air Lines	08/12/88
1534	49653	-82	N478AA	American Airlines	22/11/88
1535	49654	-82	N479AA	American Airlines	28/11/88
1536	49655	-82	N480AA	American Airlines	30/11/88
1537	49511	-82	B2127	SAIC 12/China Eastern	12/89
1538	49626	-83	EC-EMG	LAC	09/12/88
1539	49822	-83	F-GHEB	Air Liberté	20/12/88
1540	49823	-83	G-BPSC	BIA	23/12/88
1541	49587	-87	HB-IUC	CTA	16/12/88
1542	49709	-83	F-GGMC	Minerve	05/12/88
1543	49615	-82	DE-DID	SAS	08/12/88
1544	49549	-82	I-DAVP	ATI	19/12/88
1545	49656	-82	N481AA	American Airlines	12/12/88
1546	49675	-82	N482AA	American Airlines	16/12/88
1547	49710	-83	XA-TOR	Lineas Aereas La Tur	15/12/88
1548	49512	-82	B2128	SAIC 13/China Northern	12/89
1549	49724	-87	N801ML	Midway Airlines	29/03/89
1550	49676	-82	N483AA	American Airlines	20/12/88
1551	49677	-82	N484AA	American Airlines	21/12/88
1552	49725	-87	N802ML	Midway Airlines	30/03/98
1553	49728	-82	SE-DIE	SAS	24/02/89
1554	49824	-83	9Y-THU	BWIA International	23/12/88
1555	49678	-82	N485AA	American Airlines	13/01/89
1556	49614	-87	OY-KHI	SAS	03/03/89
1557	49679	-82	N486AA	American Airlines	20/01/89
1558	49680	-82	N487AA	American Airlines	25/01/89
1559	49769	-83	D-ALLK	Aero Lloyd	01/02/89
1560	49681	-82	N488AA	American Airlines	30/01/89
1561	49708	-83	XA-TUR	Lineas Aereas La Tur	28/02/89
1562	49682	-82	N489AA	American Airlines	08/02/89
1563	49683	-82	N490AA	American Airlines	06/02/89
1564	49684	-82	N491AA	American Airlines	22/02/89
1565	49730	-82	N492AA	American Airlines	15/02/89
1566	49731	-82	N493AA	American Airlines	13/02/89
1567	49732	-82	N494AA	American Airlines	21/02/89
1568	49513	-82	B2129	SAIC 14/China Eastern	12/89
1569	49606	-87	SE-DIF	SAS	02/03/89
1570	49719	-88	N932DL	Delta Air Lines	24/03/89
1571	49720	-88	N933Dl	Delta Air Lines	11/03/89
1572	49608	-87	SE-DIH	SAS	31/03/89
1573	49845	-83	D-AGWA	German Wings	27/03/89
1574	49721	-88	N934DL	Delta Air Lines	15/03/89
1575	49722	-88	N935DL	Delta Air Lines	25/03/89
1576	49723	-88	N936DL	Delta Air Lines	28/04/89
1577	49825	-83	N940AS	Alaska Airlines	31/03/89
1579	49844	-81	HB-ISX	Swissair	31/03/89
1580	49627	-83	EC-EQZ	Spanair	25/04/89
1581	49846	-83	D-AGWB	German Wings	30/03/89
1582	49628	-83	EC-EOM	Oasis International	25/04/89
1583	49629	-83	EC-EOY	Oasis International	15/05/89

Fuselage No	Serial No	Model	Registration	Operator	Delivery
1584	49550	-82	I-DAVR	ATI	24/04/89
1585	49847	-83	D-AGWC	German Wings	10/05/89
1586	49551	-82	I-DAVS	ATI	01/05/89
1587	49767	-87	D-ALLI	Aero Lloyd	05/05/89
1588	49810	-88	N937DL	Delta Air Lines	20/05/89
1589	49514	-82	B2130	SAIC 15/China Northern	12/89
1590	49811	-88	N938DL	Delta Air Lines	26/05/89
1591	49630	-83	EC-216	Spanair	01/06/89
1592	49848	-83	D-AGWD	German Wings	22/05/89
1593	49812	-88	N939DL	Delta Air Lines	26/05/89
1594	49877	-83	OH-LMT	Finnair	28/05/89
1595	49768	-87	D-ALLJ	Aero Lloyd	07/06/89
1596	496331	-83	EC-EPM	Oasis International	14/06/89
1597	49552	-82	I-DAVT	ATI	08/06/89
1598	49820	-81	JA8294	Japan Air System	16/06/89
1599	49813	-88	N940DL	Delta Air Lines	17/06/89
1600	49794	-82	I-DAWU	ATI	20/06/89
1601	49854	-83	D-ALLL	Aero Lloyd	19/06/89
1602	49814	-88	N941DL	Delta Air Lines	12/07/89
1603	49632	-83	9Y-THV	BWIA International	11/07/89
1604	49465	-87	JA8279	Japan Air System	28/07/89
1605	49815	-88	N942DL	Delta Air Lines	19/07/89
1606	49759	-88	N156PL	Midway Airlines	21/12/89
1607	49733	-82	N495AA	American Airlines	12/07/89
1608	49816	-88	N943DL	Delta Air Lines	02/08/89
1609	49515	-82	B2131	SAIC 16/China Eastern	12/12/89
1610	49726	-87	N803ML	Midway Airlines	19/07/89
1611	49618	-83	F-GGMD	Minerve	21/07/89
1612	49817	-88	N944DL	Delta Air Lines	12/08/89
1613	49818	-88	N945DL	Delta Air Lines	23/08/89
1614	49706	-87	SE-DHI	Transwede Airlines	05/09/89
1615	49821	-81	JA8295	Japan Air System	12/08/89
1616	49925	-82	N941AS	Alaska Airlines	16/08/89
1617	49641	-87	HB-IUD	CTA	18/08/89
1618	49740	-82	I-SMEP	Alisarda	21/08/89
1619	49734	-82	N496AA	American Airlines	18/08/89
1620	49760	-88	N157PL	Midwest Express	01/12/89
1621	49727	-87	M804ML	Midway Airlines	10/09/89
1622	49516	-82	B2132	SAIC 17/China Northern	27/02/90
1623	49761	-88	N158L	Aeromexico	30/11/89
1624	49762	-88	N601ME	Midwest Express	17/11/89
1625	49909	-81	SE-DIL	SAS	30/08/89
1626	49763	-88	N160PL	Aeromexico	30/11/89
1627	49784	-83	N509MD	Austral Lineas Aereas	05/09/89
1628	49785	-83	HL7271	Korean Air Lines	14/09/89
1629	49819	-88	N946DL	Delta Air Lines	20/09/98
1630	49741	-83	OH-LMU	Finnair	23/09/89
1631	49786	-83	9Y-THW	BWIA International	19/09/89
1632	49764	-88	N161PL	Aeromexico	30/11/89
1633	49517	-82	B2133	SAIC18/	
1634	49777	-87	N805ML	Midway Airlines	27/09/89
1635	49735	-82	N497AA	American Airlines	26/09/89
1636	49787	-83	HL7274	Korean Air Lines	28/09/89

Fuselage No	Serial No	Model	Registration	Operator	Delivery
1637	49663	-83	G-PATD	Paramount Airways	29/09/89
1638	49910	-81	OY-KHK	SAS	29/09/89
1639	49795	-82	I-DAVV	Alitalia	12/10/89
1640	49736	-82	N498AA	American Airlines	06/10/89
1641	49737	-82	N499AA	American Airlines	12/10/89
1642	49789	-83	9Y-THX	BWIA International	20/10/89
1643	49790	-83	EC-307	Spanair	24/10/89
1644	49791	-83	F-ODTN	Aerocancun	30/10/89
1645	49765	-88	N162PL	Aeromexico	01/12/89
1646	49778	-87	N806ML	Midway Airlines	09/11/89
1647	49518	-82	B2134	SAIC 19/China Northern	03/04/90
1648	49738	-82	N501AA	American Airlines	30/10/89
1649	49739	-82	N33502	American Airlines	31/10/89
1651	49798	-82	N70504	American Airlines	31/10/89
1652	49799	-82	N505AA	American Airlines	09/11/89
1653	49911	-81	OY-KHL	SAS	17/11/89
1654	49827	-87	EC-290	Iberia	06/04/90
1655	49792	-83	XA-RPH	Aerocancun	22/11/89
1656	49793	-83	C-GKMV	Minerve Canada	01/12/89
1657	49766	-88	N163PL	Midway Airlines	21/12/89
1658	49519	-82	B	SAIC 20/China Eastern	05/06/90
1659	49912	-81	LN-RMJ	SAS	01/12/89
1660	49800	-82	N7506	American Airlines	04/12/89
1661	49801	-82	N3507A	American Airlines	04/12/89
1662	49802	-82	N7608	American Airlines	20/12/89
1663	49803	-82	N7509	American Airlines	11/12/89
1664	49878	-88	N947DL	Delta Air Lines	21/12/89
1665	49913	-81	SE-DIL	SAS	15/12/89
1666	49879	-88	N948DL	Delta Air Lines	29/12/89
1667	49828	-87	EC-EUD	Iberia	04/04/90
1668	49968	-83	F-GHEI	Air Liberté	26/02/90
1669	49804	-82	N510AM	American Airlines	15/12/89
1670	49779	-87	N807ML	Midway Airlines	27/12/89
1671	49520	-82	B2136	SAIC 21/	17/09/90
1672	49805	-82	N90511	American Airlines	27/12/89
1673	49806	-82	N7512A	American Airlines	27/12/89
1674	49780	-87	N808ML	Midway Airlines	10/01/90
1675	49856	-83	D-ALLM	Aero Lloyd	06/02/90
1676	49880	-88	N949DL	Delta Air Lines	09/02/90
1677	49881	-88	N950DL	Delta Air Lines	21/02/90
1678	49829	-87	EC-EUC	Iberia	04/90
1679	49882	-88	N951DL	Delta Air Lines	23/02/90
1680	49904	-83	OH-LMV	Finnair	23/02/90
1681	49413	-87	OE-LMM	Austrian Airlines	/90
1682	49414	-87	OE-LMN	Austrian Airlines	/90
1683	49883	-88	N952DL	Delta Air Lines	09/03/90
1684	49830	-87	EC-EUL	Iberia	12/04/90
1685	49884	-88	N953DL	Delta Air Lines	21/03/90
1686	49890	-82	N513AA	American Airlines	08/03/90
1687	49857	-83	D-ALLN	Aero Lloyd	30/03/90
1688	49831	-87	EC-EVB	Iberia	27/04/90
1689	49885	-88	N954DL	Delta Air Lines	28/03/90
1690	49521	-82	B2137	SAIC 22/	05/09/90

Fuselage No	Serial No	Model	Registration	Operator	Delivery
1691	49886	-88	N955DL	Delta Air Lines	31/03/90
1692	49888	-87	OE-LMO	Austrian Airlines	/90
1693	44914	-81	OY-KHM	SAS	/90
1694	49891	-82	N7514A	American Airlines	27/03/90
1695	49892	-82	N3515	American Airlines	31/03/90
1696	49883	-82	N5116AM	American Airlines	31/03/90
1697	49894	-82	N7517A	American Airlines	30/03/90
1698	49895	-82	N7518A	American Airlines	30/03/90
1699	49887	-88	N956DL	Delta Air Lines	27/04/90
1700	49976	-88	N957DL	Delta Air Lines	28/04/90
1701	49977	-88	N958DL	Delta Air Lines	03/05/90
1702	49522	-82	B2138	SAIC 23/	03/10/90
1703	49832	-87	EC-EXF	Iberia	31/05/90
1704	53050	-83	EC-EUZ	Aviaco	07/05/90
1705	49610	-87	LN-RMK	SAS	
1706	49833	-87	EC-EXG	Iberia	29/05/90
1707	49896	-82	N7519A	American Airlines	14/05/90
1708	49897	-82	N7520A	American Airlines	10/05/90
1709	49898	-82	N7521A	American Airlines	17/05/90
1710	49978	-88	N959DL	Delta Air Lines	24/05/90
1711	49979	-88	N960DL	Delta Air Lines	15/06/90
1712	49980	-88	N961DL	Delta Air Lines	31/05/90
1713	49796	-82	I-DAVW	ATI	29/05/90
1714	49834	-87	EC-EXR	Iberia	20/06/90
1715	49926	-88	XA-AMS	Aeromexico	31/05/90
1716	49927	-88	XA-AMT	Aeromexico	31/05/90
1717	49835	-87	EC-EXM	Iberia	22/06/90
1718	53051	-83	EC-EVU	Aviaco	14/06/90
1719	49969	-82	I-DAVX	Alitalia	14/06/90
1720	49930	-83	HB-ISZ	Balair	20/06/90
1721	49836	-87	EC-EXN	Iberia	02/07/90
1722	49899	-82	N7522A	American Airlines	20/06/90
1723	49915	-82	N59523	American Airlines	21/06/90
1724	49523	-82	B2139	SAIC 24/	04/12/90
1725	49981	-88	N962DL	Delta Air Lines	27/07/90
1726	49982	-88	N963DL	Delta Air LInes	28/06/90
1727	49466	-87	JA8280	Japan Air System	29/06/90
1728	49855	-83	F-GGME	Minerve	29/06/90
1729	49916	-82	N70524	American Airlines	28/06/90
1730	49837	-87	EC-EXT	Iberia	24/07/90
1731	53052	-83	N942AS	Alaska Airlines	18/07/90
1732	49928	-88	XA-AMU	Aeromexico	20/07/90
1733	49838	-87	EC-EYB	Iberia	06/????
1734	49907	-81	JA8296	Japan Air System	20/????
1735	49917	-82	N7525A	American Airlines	26/07/90
1736	53012	-83	D-ALLO	Aero Lloyd	28/07/90
1737	49970	-82	I-DAVZ	ATI	31/07/90
1738	53013	-83	D-ALLP	Aero Lloyd	30/07/90
1739	49839	-87	EC-EYX	Iberia	16/08/90
1740	53014	-83	D-ALLQ	Aero Lloyd	13/08/90
1741	49929	-88	XA-AMV	Aeromexico	10/08/90
1742					
1743	49918	-82	N7526A	American Airlines	16/08/90

Fuselage No	Serial No	Model	Registration	Operator	Delivery
1744	49919	-82	N7527A	American Airlines	22/08/90
1745	49840	-87	EC-EYY	Iberia	30/08/90
1746	49524	-82	B2140	SAIC 25/	08/01/90
1747	49983	-88	N964DL	Delta Air Lines	14/09/90
1748	49984	-88	N965DL	Delta Air Lines	24/08/90
1749	49908	-81	JA8297	Japan Air System	28/08/90
1750	49920	-82	N7528A	American Airlines	05/09/90
1751	49841	-87	EC-EYZ	Iberia	26/09/90
1752	49921	-82	N70529	American Airlines	04/09/90
1753	49922	-82	N7530	American Airlines	12/09/90
1754	49931	-82	N809ML	Midway Airlines	12/09/90
1755	49971	-82	I-DACM	ATI	15/09/90
1756	49932	-82	N810ML	Midway Airlines	24/09/90
1757	49972	-82	I-DACN	ATI	14/09/90
1758	49923	-82	N7531A	American Airlines	19/09/90
1759	49924	-82	N7532A	American Airlines	24/09/90
1760	49987	-82	N7533A	American Airlines	26/09/90
1761	49889	-82	N811ML	Midway Airlines	27/09/90
1762	49973	-82	I-DAC	ATI	27/09/90
1763	49842	-87	EC-EZA	Iberia	30/09/90
1764	49934	-83	N907MD	Austral	29/09/90
1765	49900	-82	N6202D	Unifly	28/09/90
1766	49901	-82	N6202S	Unifly	28/09/90
1767	49905	-82	OH-LMW	Finnair	02/10/90
1768	49988	-82	N7534A	American Airlines	30/09/90
1769	49989	-82	N7535A	American Airlines	22/10/90
1770	49990	-82	N7536A	American Airlines	23/10/90
1771	49843	-87	EC-EZS	Iberia	31/10/90
1772					
1773	49935	-83	G-DCAC	Airtours International	19/11/90
1774	49974	-82	I-DACQ	ATI	26/10/90
1775	49975	-82	I-DACR	ATI	31/10/90
1776	53044	-83	N905ML	Midway Airlines	30/10/90
1777	53045	-83	N906ML	Midway Airlines	31/10/90
1778	49936	-83	G-HCRP	Airtours International	19/11/90
1779	53018	-83	N943AS	Alaska Airlines	05/11/90
1780	49991	-82	N7537A	American Airlines	31/10/90
1781	49992	-82	N7538A	American Airlines	08/11/90
1782	49993	-82	N7539A	American Airlines	13/11/90
1783	53019	-83	N944AS	Alaska Airlines	13/11/90

Swissair's OH-LMH, an MD-82. *Chris Doggett*

Fuselage No	Serial No	Model	Registration	Operator	Delivery
1784	49937	-83	G-COES	Airtours International	21/01/90
1785	49938	-83	XA-RTK	La Tur	18/12/90
1786	49906	-82	OH-LMX	Finnair	15/11/90
1787	49939	-83	EI-CBR	Irish Aerospace	03/12/90
1788	49940	-83	G-TTPT	Airtours International	28/12/90
1789	53020	-83	N947AS	Alaska Airlines	07/12/90
1790	49994	-82	N7540A	American Airlines	04/12/90
1791	49995	-82	N7541A	American Airlines	05/12/90
1792	49996	-82	N7542A	American Airlines	10/12/90
1793	49941	-83	G-JSMC	Airtours International	14/12/90
1794	53046	-83	N907ML	Midway Airlines	03/12/90
1795	53115	-88	N966DL	Delta Air Lines	12/12/90
1796	53116	-88	N967DL	Delta Air Lines	14/12/90
1797	53017	-82	N812ML	Midway Airlines	14/12/90
1798					
1799	49942	-83	EI-CBS	Irish Aerospace	04/12/90
1800	49998	-81	SE-DIX	SAS	18/12/90
1801	53021	-83	N948AS	Alaska Airlines	21/12/90
1802	53025	-82	N7543A	American Airlines	18/12/90
1803	49999	-81	SE-DIN	SAS	21/12/90
1804	53026	-82	N7544A	American Airlines	19/12/90
1805	53027	-82	N16545	American Airlines	18/12/90
1806	53053	-82	I-DACS	Alitalia	21/12/90

MD-90-30 FUSELAGE INDEX

Fuselage No	Serial No	Registration	Operator	Delivery
2018	53367	N901DC	McDonnell Douglas	13/02/93
2094	53382	N902DA	Delta Airlines	24/02/95
2095	53383	N903DA	Delta Airlines	26/03/95
2096	53384	N904DA	Delta Airlines	24/03/95
2097	53385	N905DA	Delta Airlines	29/04/95
2098	53352	JA8062	Japan Air System	12/07/96
2099	53386	N906DA	Delta Airlines	22/07/95
2100	53381	N902DA	Delta Airlines	27/08/93
2115	53387	N907DA	Delta Airlines	17/08/95
2117	53388	N908DA	Delta Airlines	27/09/95
2120	53353	JA8063	Japan Air System	03/07/96
2122	53389	N909DA	Delta Airlines	28/10/95
2123	53390	N910DN	Delta Airlines	18/11/95
2125	53354	JA8064	Japan Air System	06/01/96
2126	53391	N911DA	Delta Airlines	17/12/95
2129	53489	N901RA	Reno Air	15/03/96
2131	53355	JA8065	Japan Air System	18/03/96
2133	53490	N902RA	Reno Air	28/03/96
2136	53392	N912DN	Delta Airlines	25/04/96
2138	53457	SE-DMF	Scandinavian Airlines	16/10/96
2140	53458	OY-KIL	Scandinavian Airlines	02/11/96
2141	53459	LN-ROA	Scandinavian Airlines	14/11/96
2142	53460	OY-KIM	Scandinavian Airlines	21/12/96
2143	53523	B2250	China Northern	28/07/96

Fuselage No	Serial No	Registration	Operator	Delivery
2144	53551	N903RA	Reno Air	30/07/96
2146	53524	B2251	China Northern	28/08/96
2147	53461	SE-DMG	Scandinavian Airlines	02/12/96
2149	53462	LN-ROB	Scandinavian Airlines	21/12/96
2150	53525	B2252	China Northern	01/09/96
2153	53534	B-16901	Eva Airways Corp	30/10/96
2154	53393	N913DN	Delta Airlines	21/10/96
2156	53394	N914DN	Delta Airlines	08/11/96
2157	53356	JA8066	Japan Air System	31/10/96
2158	53535	B-17911	Eva Airways Corp	25/11/96
2159	53395	N915DN	Delta Airlines	22/11/96
2160	53536	B-17912	Eva Airways Corp	27/11/96
2161	53396	N916DN	Delta Airlines	13/12/96
2162	53537	B-17913	Eva Airways Corp	14/12/96
2163	53552	TC-KTA	KTHY	27/03/97
2164	53357	JA8069	Japan Air System	27/12/96
2165	53553	TC-KTB	KTHY	29/03/97
2166	53554	TC-KTC	KTHY	
2168	53538	B-17915	Unit Airways Corp	28/01/97
2169	53567	B-15301	Great China Airlines	18/03/97
2170	53526	B-2253	China Northern	24/02/97
2171	53568	B-16902	EVA Airways Corp	25/04/97
2172	53539	B-17916	Uni Airways Corp	06/03/97
2173	53569			
2175	53527	B-2254	China Northern	21/03/97
2177	53528	B-2255	China Northern	10/04/97
2179	53358	JA8070	Japan Air System	03/05/97
2181	53570	N904RA	Reno Air	08/12/97
2182	53573	N905RA	Reno Air	12/12/97
2184	53374			
2190	53360	JA8020	Japan Air System	29/07/97
2191	53491	HZ-APA	Saudi Arabian	
2193	53571	B-17918	Eva Airways Corp	31/07/97
2194	53543	SE-DMH	Scandinavian Airlines	31/07/97
2195	53576	SU-BMQ	AMC Aviation, Egypt	31/07/97
2196	53359	JA8004	Japan Air System	
2197	53544	OY-KIN	Scandinavian Airlines	27/07/97
2198	53582	B-2256	China Eastern	09/10/97
2200		B-	China Eastern	09/10/97
2202	53583	B-2257	China Eastern	09/10/97
2203	53584	B-2258	China Eastern	16/12/97
2205	53492	HZ-APB	Saudi Arabian	
2207	53555	JA001D	Japan Air System	
2209	53493	HZ-APC	Saudi Arabina	
2210	53556	JA002D	Japan Air System	19/12/97
2211		JA003D	Japan Air System	26/12/97

9 CHRONOLOGY

20 Oct 1977	MDC announces start of 'Super 80' programme.
16 April 1979	MD-82 announced.
June 1979	FAA Certification awarded to the JT8D-209 engine.
18 Oct 1979	First flight of prototype MD-80.
26 Aug 1980	Type Certificate amendment covering DC-9-81 (MD-81) variant.
12 Sept 1980	First MD-80 delivered to Swissair.
5 Oct 1980	First MD-80 enters commercial service with Swissair.
8 Jan 1981	First flight of MD-82.
31 July 1981	MD-82 certificated.
Aug 1981	First MD-82 enters service with Republic Airlines.
1 Dec 1981	First fatal crash of an MD-82. YU-ANA belonging to Inex Adria crashes into Mont St Pietro, Corsica. 180 fatalities, no survivors.
26 Aug 1982	Last DC-9 series airliner completed.
28 Oct 1982	US Navy took receipt of last DC-9-32 built.
31 Jan 1983	MD-83 announced – formally called the DC-9-80 (Super 80).
17 Dec 1984	First flight of MD-83.
12 April 1985	Agreement with General Administration of Civil Aviation of China (CAAC) for purchase of 26 MD-80s (25 to be assembled in Shanghai).
July 1985	First MD-83 enters service with Finnair.
12 Dec 1985	First delivery to CAAC of MDC-built MD-82.
4 Dec 1986	First MD-87 flight.

ABOVE: MD-82 YU-ANC is seen in Adria livery in the early 1990s. After two changes of registration, many leases and sub-leases, it became SX-BBW with Venus Airlines on 4 April 1995. *Chris Doggett*

BELOW LEFT: Paramount Airways, based at Bristol in the UK, operated a total of four MD-83s on lease from the GPA Group between April 1987 and August 1989. Unfortunately the airline encountered difficulties and a rescue package failed. This is G-PATD. *Chris Doggett*

17 June 1987	UHB prototype flight trials begin with General Electric GE36.
2 July 1987	First flight of Shanghai-assembled MD-82.
15 Aug 1987	First flight of MD-88.
21 Oct 1987	DC-9-87 (MD-87) certificated.
Nov 1987	First MD-87s enter service with Austrian Airlines and Finnair.
10 Dec 1987	MD-88 certificated.
5 Jan 1988	First MD-88 enters service with Delta.
13 April 1989	In UHB trials, first flight with Pratt & Whitney-Allison 578-DX. Howevere, UHB development had to be abandoned shortly afterwards.
14 Nov 1989	MD-90 series launched.
23 March 1992	1,000th MD-80 series airliner delivered.
11 June 1992	2,000th Douglas twin-jet airliner delivered to (American Airlines).
25 June 1992	Order approved for 20 MD-80s and 20 MD-90s (most 'Trunkliners') for China, plus options. Later renegotiated to 20 MDC-built MD-90s.
22 Feb 1993	First flight of the MD-90.
Aug 1994	MDC offers new MD-95 twin-jet airliner (first announced 1991).
16 Nov 1994	MD-90 certificated.
Nov 1994	MD-95 presented to potential customers.
1995	Long Beach celebrates the 75th anniversary of the founding of the Douglas Aircraft Company.
24 Feb 1995	First MD-90 delivered to Delta.
1 April 1995	First MD-90 in service.
Autumn 1995	Valujet orders 50 MD-95-30 airliners with option for 50 more.
27 May 1997	Final assembly starts on MD-95-30
28 April 1997	First run of BMW Rolls-Royce BR715 engine for MD-95.
4 Aug 1997	MDC Long Beach becomes the Douglas Products Division of the Boeing Commercial Aircraft Group for $15b.
May 1988	Bavaria Int Lease Co becomes first European customer for 717-200
10 June 1998	First 717-200 (MD-95) rolled out at Long Beach.
2 Sept 1998	First flight of 717-200 from Long Beach

INDEX